Praise for *Enjoying God in Everything*

DeWitt focuses on beauty and how we can enjoy God in everything. Yes, everything. He wants Christians to enjoy beauty and joy and wonder and to allow each of these things to lead us to the source of all that is good, true, and beautiful. I am glad to commend it to you.

TIM CHALLIES
Blogger at Challies.com

To fulfill our primary purpose—enjoying and glorifying God forever—we need the eyes to see the beauty of God, the beauty of what He has made, and the beauty of everything He is redeeming in Jesus Christ. Because of his exceptional capacity to perceive divine beauty, Steve DeWitt's latest book will help us all to experience more of life's deepest, purest pleasures and then give God the praise.

PHILIP RYKEN
President, Wheaton College

This book was a delightful read; it is the only book I have ever read that describes as best we can the beauty of God. By the time I was finished reading it, I found myself worshiping God and seeing Him in places I had never seen Him before. Give yourself a break from the noise around you; read this book and contemplate our great God!

ERWIN W. LUTZER
Pastor Emeritus, The Moody Church, Chicago

Steve DeWitt's new book, *Enjoying God in Everything*, is an invitation to explore the beauty of God expressed through creation and Christ in a way that leads us to greater wonder and worship. Like a refreshing drink on a hot day, this book reminds us to sit and savor all the loveliness of God as we gaze upon His goodness.

MELISSA KRUGER
Author and director of Women's Initiatives for The Gospel Coalition

Why are you naturally drawn to beauty? What if it were possible to get even more joy and delight from your experiences of beauty? How might you experience this joy and delight all the time, in even the most ordinary parts of your life and our world? DeWitt addresses these important questions in this accessible and eminently quotable book. Indeed, what you have in your hands is a thoughtful and practical roadmap to a richer engagement with beauty by way of seeing more clearly the God who is the source of all beauty.

VERMON PIERRE
Lead Pastor, Roosevelt Community Church

Enjoying God in Everything will point you to what you really want—beyond the beauties and wonders of this world to the beauty of God Himself, the One we long for and love. Steve DeWitt places our cravings for beauty and joy within the biblical story and shows us what a life of joy in God's goodness looks like.

TREVIN WAX
Vice President of Research and Resource Development at the North American Mission Board; visiting professor at Wheaton College; author of *The Thrill of Orthodoxy, Rethink Your Self,* and *This Is Our Time*

Trying to grasp the meaning of God's beauty is a heady exercise, but Steve De-Witt has the rare ability to explain and illustrate complex concepts in a way that is precise and even whimsical. This is my favorite book on the beauty of God—reading it will make your heart soar! It is a must-read for students of Scripture and anyone who wants to go deep in their understanding of the nature of God.

RICK THOMPSON
President, Global Action

As Steve DeWitt rightly says in this simple yet profound book, the more we grow in our understanding of and delight in the source and goal of beauty, the more we will grow in our wonder and worship of God. For God is the creator, sustainer, and consummator of all things true, good, and beautiful. And I can't think of a time where this call to behold the beauty of God is more needed. Our beautiful God, who created beautiful things, especially the beautiful gospel of Jesus Christ, changes everything.

JULIUS J. KIM
President, The Gospel Coalition

Enjoying God in Everything

A Guide to Maximizing Life's Pleasures

STEVE DEWITT

MOODY PUBLISHERS
CHICAGO

This book is an abridged adaptation of Steve DeWitt, *Eyes Wide Open: Enjoying God in Everything* (Grand Rapids: Credo House Publishers, 2012).

Edited by Connor Sterchi
Interior and cover design: Erik M. Peterson
Cover photo of coffee with landscape copyright © 2022 by Onchira Wongsiri/Shutterstock (774119458). All rights reserved.

Library of Congress Cataloging-in-Publication Data

Names: DeWitt, Steve (Senior Pastor), author.
Title: Enjoying God in everything : a guide to maximizing life's pleasures / Steve DeWitt.
Description: Chicago : Moody Publishers, [2022] | "This book is an abridged adaptation of Steve DeWitt, Eyes Wide Open: Enjoying God in Everything (Grand Rapids: Credo House Publishers, 2012)." | Includes bibliographical references. | Summary: "We were made by God but also for Him and His beauty. Pastor Steve DeWitt invites us to taste and see how God is the beauty behind all beauty. DeWitt opens our eyes to beauty's appointed end: worship! Nothing is more desirable than the beautiful one who saves: Jesus Christ"-- Provided by publisher.
Identifiers: LCCN 2022016622 (print) | LCCN 2022016623 (ebook) | ISBN 9780802429278 (paperback) | ISBN 9780802473912 (ebook)
Subjects: LCSH: God (Christianity)--Worship and love. | Desire for God. | Aesthetics--Religious aspects--Christianity. | God (Christianity)--Omnipresence. | Happiness--Religious aspects--Christianity. | BISAC: RELIGION / Christian Living / Personal Growth | RELIGION / Christian Ministry / Discipleship
Classification: LCC BV4817 .D48 2022 (print) | LCC BV4817 (ebook) | DDC 231.7--dc23/eng/20220519
LC record available at https://lccn.loc.gov/2022016622
LC ebook record available at https://lccn.loc.gov/2022016623

Originally delivered by fleets of horse-drawn wagons, the affordable paperbacks from D. L. Moody's publishing house resourced the church and served everyday people. Now, after more than 125 years of publishing and ministry, Moody Publishers' mission remains the same—even if our delivery systems have changed a bit. For more information on other books (and resources) created from a biblical perspective, go to www.moodypublishers.com or write to:

Moody Publishers
820 N. LaSalle Boulevard
Chicago, IL 60610

1 3 5 7 9 10 8 6 4 2

Printed in the United States of America

It is my joy to dedicate this book to each elder, pastor,
and leader with whom I have served in pastoral ministry at
College Park Church (1992–1997) and Bethel Church (1997–present).
God has used you in profound ways in my life and I am forever grateful.
Soli Deo Gloria.

Contents

Introduction

Splendor and majesty are before Him,
strength and beauty are in His sanctuary.
PSALM 96:6 (NASB)

If someone is very well known, it is often said they need no introduction. This book will not introduce you to beauty. You have been thrilled by the beautiful your whole life. So have I. Perhaps we share something else in common. Much of my life has been motivated by wonders big and small, yet I have not known why. My passion for all things beautiful is a puzzle. I am a beauty junkie. I love sunsets on the ocean (or my pretend local ocean, Lake Michigan), mountain view vistas, guitar licks, and my wife's strawberry pie.

Our cravings are undeniable. Where did they come from? Why are these so universal to the human experience?

My purpose in this book is to help you understand the why of the wow so that your pleasures may be even richer and deeper. Financial advisers speak with cautionary tone about "opportunity costs," when not investing keeps our returns from being as great as they could be. The opportunity costs for not relishing beauty in the right ways and for the right reasons are substantial and possibly even eternal. This book is a guide to maximizing our delight in the beautiful by intensifying our wonder and worship.

We are not the first to find mystery in our yearnings for more and better wonder. The ancients did too. The more reflective and philosophical of them saw beauty, along with truth and goodness, as the goal of life's pursuits. The remnants of their writings and constructions whisper this: the geometric precision of Stonehenge, the astonishing symmetry of the pyramids of Giza, the *Pietà*, the *Iliad*, Parthenon, Great Wall, Bach's *St Matthew Passion*, and a certain genius of language from Stratford-upon-Avon. This list could go on and on. The wonders of the ancient world resemble the passions of our modern world. C. S. Lewis speaks for all of us: "The sweetest thing in all my life has been the longing . . . to find the place where all the beauty came from."[1]

The technical term for all this is *aesthetics*, the philosophy of art and culture. Think of a beautiful moment in your life. What was your internal experience? How would you describe it? Perhaps you would use a word like staggering, moving, breathtaking, or even spiritual. I prefer the term *wonder*. We will explore wonder in this book—what it is, why we like it, and how to amplify it.

The thesis of this book is that God has so wired us that beauty generates powerful experiences of wonder. Wonder is one of God's most precious gifts to us, especially when it leads us to its intended end—worship of our beautiful God. Should we be surprised to discover that the beautiful God made beautiful things to affect us and bless us? Like a friend who invites us to enjoy the food of a new restaurant or listen to a favorite song, God invites us into His own delight in divine beauty. His invitations are all around us. As John Calvin noted, "There is no portion of the world, however minute, that does not exhibit at least some sparks of beauty; while it is impossible to contemplate the vast and beautiful fabric as it extends around, without being overwhelmed by the immense weight of glory."[2] Or Cornelius Plantinga, "Ultimate Beauty comes not *from* a lover or a landscape or a home, but only *through* them."[3]

When we turn the wonder beauty creates back toward God with worship, these sparks can and should light our souls on fire. As the Puritan pastor Charles Simeon said, "There are but two lessons for the Christian to learn: the one is to enjoy God in every thing; the other is to enjoy every thing in God."[4] When we do, our worship enhances our pleasure in the beautiful, which further increases our wonder and fuels greater thanksgiving to God.

The second half of the book provides practical help for enjoying God in the day-to-day of life, through what He has made and through what we make. Both are precious gifts *if* we allow the wonder they generate to lead us to worship. May your time in these pages enhance all your aesthetical experiences by enlarging your view of God as the ultimate Beauty behind all beauty. Understanding how God wired me for beauty has brought experiential and soul-filling meaning to the moments of beauty He so graciously gives me. I was made for beauty. So were you.

Chapter 1

The Beauty of God

One day I was waiting for a flight in Concourse C of Chicago's Midway Airport. I had time to mill around, with my coffee in hand, and people watch. Chicago's musical scene regularly welcomes the best musicians in the world. As I walked by the restroom area, I heard a lovely sound emanating from the women's bathroom. From a bathroom? Yes, a violin was being played by a very skilled violinist. Who was she? I sat down near the door to enjoy this impromptu concert. She kept playing and playing. I saw women coming out of the restroom with strange looks on their faces. What they saw and heard was an unfamiliar experience.

As she continued to play, I was transfixed. It was beautiful. Eventually, my flight had to leave, and I left not knowing the musician behind the wall. I would have liked to meet her and thank her. I have told and written about this in other places.

One day I received a letter from someone on the East Coast who heard of my airport violin story and told me they have a friend who is a concert violinist and regularly practices in airport bathrooms because of the acoustics. Perhaps it was her!

This story illustrates the spiritual challenge beauty presents. We see, hear, taste, touch, and smell created loveliness. It envelopes us every day. We delight in the pleasures big and small. But where did they come from? Who or what made them? What do they tell us of the One who created them?

The psalmist wrote, "The heavens declare the glory of God, and the sky above proclaims his handiwork. Day to day pours out speech, and night to night reveals knowledge. There is no speech, nor are there words, whose voice is not heard" (Ps. 19:1–3).

Discovering the beauty of God generally requires working backward from the created to the Creator. The psalmist urges us to look up to the sky and the stars. The preaching voice of the galaxies is materially declaring a spiritual truth: God is glorious, majestic, and excellent. Similarly, the prophet Isaiah has a heavenly vision and records for us the seraphim's antiphonal chant, "Holy, holy, holy is the LORD of hosts; the whole earth is full of his glory!" (Isa. 6:3).

How is a created material planet filled with the glory of a spiritual God? We look in vain for the same kind of visible glory seen during the exodus or in the face of the transfigured Christ. The earthly glory the angels celebrate is creation as a reflection of the worth of divine majesty. It is symbolic worth, as wedding rings are emblematic of something much deeper and more valuable. Creation is God's self-portrait.

I have two young daughters. My wife, Jennifer, and I fulfilled a long desire this year by having a portrait painted of our beloved daughters. The artist amazed us. We sent her pictures of our girls. She never met any of us. Yet what she did with brush and canvas so closely resembles them that friends thought the painting was a

14

photo. The accuracy of the portrait is not lost on me either. When it comes to my daughters, I am the stereotypical doting and blubbering father. Before we received the painting, the artist sent us video footage of her painting it and the finished product. I watched the video over and over again, tearful each time. Why? Because of the paint and canvas, colors and shapes? No, I wept because what she created so visually resembled those I love; my heart went from the creation to the object of the creation. I treasured the art because I love the subjects of the art.

THE DIVINE PORTRAIT

Creation is not God. That would be pantheism. Rather, creation is God's self-portrait. I wouldn't mistake a painting for my daughters. Yet many have mistaken creation—God's stunning self-portrait—for God Himself.

Creation is magnificent in scale, symmetry, balance, depth, variety, and harmony. These descriptions apply in every dimension, element, particle, and galaxy. God's self-portrait is multidimensional, a diverse spectrum of color and sound and wonder, reflecting His beauty and character. The universe's scale, scope, and symmetry are a finite indication of God's infinite worth. What do we call such majesty? We call it the beauty of God. God defines beauty by His very essence, as He is the source and standard of all beauty. He is the measure of morality, truth, love, as well as their absence—evil, hate, injustice, and falsehood.

Yet the concept of God's beauty can be challenging. For one thing, God is spirit (John 4:24; 2 Cor. 3:17). We are limited in our ability to understand God's beauty in that our experience of beauty is essentially sensory. We cannot see God or smell God or touch God. He is "the invisible God" (Col. 1:15). Yet this invisible

God chose to express the fullness of His beauty in physical ways. The spectacle is not the beauty itself. We must not confuse God's expression of His beauty with its essential character. The created world is an expression of God's beauty, but it is not the essence of His beauty. We are accustomed to thinking about beauty as visual; considering an invisible God as beautiful requires a definition that goes beyond the senses to the core of essential beauty.

Our second problem is with the common understanding of beauty itself. We often say, "Beauty is in the eye of the beholder." This reinforces personal preferences or social influences as the measure of what is beautiful. Studies show that we are heavily influenced by our parents' and our culture's definitions of loveliness and attractiveness. Art and architecture tend to have cultural and geographical similarities. Or consider ancient paintings of what was deemed to be feminine beauty of the past. They would never be allowed on the front cover of a glamour magazine today. Even home décor is constantly changing, and it is easy to identify which era houses were built in by their shape, look, and color. Today's beauty ends up in tomorrow's museum, or worse.

The beauty of God doesn't fit into our cultural or conditioned evaluation. God's beauty is divine, eternal, and infinite. He *is* beautiful. He always has been and eternally will be. God's beauty defies our ability to comprehend. A helpful word in grappling with divine beauty is *ineffable*. This word is one of the few that apply because it means "beyond comprehension." God transcends all aesthetic definitions. Human language cannot produce a word that adequately describes something infinitely desirable.

A popular phrase captures the ineffability of God's beauty: it blows our minds. We cannot see God's beauty (God is spirit) and we cannot comprehend it (God is infinite, and we are not).

So why even attempt to wrap our minds around the beauty of

God? For the same reason we enjoy other things that appear infinite and beyond our ability to understand completely. Why do people enjoy gazing out at the seemingly endless ocean or looking up at the starry sky?

They are visually ineffable. Still, people flock by the millions to the world's beaches. And who hasn't found themselves lost in the magnitude of the night sky?

We seek out these expressions of beauty because what we can see and comprehend draws us to wonders too awesome not to enjoy. Their ineffability entwines with their desirability. What I cannot comprehend is mysteriously interesting to me and compels me to look all the more. The same is true of God's beauty and attributes. He is more than we can know and beyond our capacity to absorb. Our finitude limits our comprehension, but what we can see draws us to wonder—which is the prelude to worship.

ATTRIBUTE OR ADJECTIVE?

Before we can understand the true essence of God's beauty, we must ask whether God's beauty is essential to God as an attribute or merely a description of God. Is it objective or subjective? This requires "seeing" past the visible to the invisible. Similar to describing a person as beautiful could mean many things. She may be beautiful in appearance like Bathsheba was beautiful. Or it could mean, as in Proverbs 31, the beauty of character.

God is beautiful both *outwardly* in His visible glory and *essentially* in the splendor of the holiness of His character. God's beauty is more than a description; it is inherent to His eternal being. We rightly describe Him as glorious and radiant, yet His beauty is core to His existence. As Jonathan Edwards describes it,

For as God is infinitely the greatest Being, so he is allowed to be infinitely the most beautiful and excellent: and all the beauty to be found throughout the whole creation is but the reflection of the diffused beams of that Being who hath an infinite fullness of brightness and glory; God . . . is the foundation and fountain of all being and all beauty.[1]

This is what the galaxies shout and what every alluring beauty in our experience declares. God is Himself beautiful and is the sum of all that is desirable. As the Beauty beyond and behind all created beauty, He is the measure of what is truly beautiful. A yardstick provides us with a simple illustration. A yardstick measures a yard and is itself a yard. God's beauty is like that. He is beauty, and He is the measure of all beauty. But God is far more than just the measure of beauty. He is the source and standard of beauty. In one sense, He is like the sun.

His beauty is essence and source, attribute and adjective. He is what all the beauties we experience flow from and reflect.

When you pick paint colors for your home, consultants advise you to look at the paint sample outside the store. Why? If you want to see the actual color, you must place the sample in sunlight. The sun is the source of light, and its rays reveal the true nature in everything else. God's beauty is like that. He is what He measures. His beauty is essence and source, attribute and adjective. He is what all the beauties we experience flow from and reflect.

THE RADIANCE OF ABSOLUTE PERFECTION

God is perfect. Think about that for a moment. He doesn't rise to the level of perfection—He is perfect. The psalmist declares,

"From Zion, perfect in beauty, God shines forth" (Ps. 50:2 NIV). God's perfection is the necessary quality of His excellence. Excellence is a qualitative attribute applied to all that God is. Second Peter 1:3 extols God as the One "who called us to his own glory and excellence." His excellence expresses His perfection, which permeates all His other attributes. God has no potential to be less perfect or more perfect. He has eternally existed, with His every quality living in absolute completeness. He cannot be anything more than He is, and He will never be anything less than He has always been. Our difficulty here is that there is nothing in our creaturely experience to adequately compare to His perfection. At best, we have meager comparisons to help us.

What is it about a sight or sound that leads you to conclude that it has inherent beauty? Let's consider a rose. Why is a rose considered beautiful? It begins with vivid color. A further look at the rose reveals the symmetrical formation, the softness of each petal, and the appearance that the rose is unveiling itself. A rose is a multisensory experience. It is delicate and fragrant. Having a bouquet of them only adds to the effect. How would a perfect rose look? There would be no deficiency to it. No petals drooping. No lack of fragrance. No browning anywhere.

How do we evaluate the perfection of a rose or anything else? It is the absence of anything lacking. That is how God is perfect. He doesn't lack anything. He is lovely in His completeness.

God's beauty is the bouquet of His perfections in His being, unveiled in His purposes and displayed in His glory.

Or consider a diamond. A diamond is viewed through its many facets. A jeweler looks at each facet to see if there are any flaws. A flaw reveals an imperfection. A flawless diamond would have no imperfect facet. If we could turn the personhood of

God before us like a diamond, we would see that every facet of His character is without flaw.

We begin to understand God's desirability by the value we place on perfection. His beauty to us is not what He lacks (nothing) but what He possesses in His character (everything). God's beauty is the bouquet of His perfections in His being, unveiled in His purposes and displayed in His glory.

TRINITARIAN WONDER

Three yet one. 1+1+1=1? This is either gibberish or a wondrous mystery. How many things can you fully understand that ever produced a "wow" in your heart? God's "three yet one" nature provides ample opportunity for wonder if we are willing to think about it on a deeper level. God's beauty is like any wonder we long to know or experience—somewhat understandable but not completely discernible.

There is no better example of this than God's threeness and His oneness. This is known in Christian theology as the doctrine of the Trinity. Although the word *Trinity* is not in Scripture, descriptions of the Godhead as one God and three persons are plentiful. Our first glimpse of plurality in unity is in Genesis 1:26, where God says, "Let *us* make man in *our* image, after *our* likeness." God is three distinct persons: the Father, the Son, and the Holy Spirit (Matt. 3:16–17; 28:19–20; 1 Cor. 8:6). This would potentially be comprehensible if Scripture stopped there. We would have three gods, a little pantheon of deities. However, these three persons are of such unity and oneness that they are in essence one God: "Hear, O Israel: The LORD our God, the LORD is one" (Deut. 6:4). God is one, and God is three. This divine relational diversity existing in harmonious unity is the core and genesis of all beauty.

God delights in this. He appraises it as inherently beautiful.

John 17 is known as Jesus' High Priestly Prayer. Here, in the upper room on the night He was betrayed, God the Son opens His heart to God the Father and gives us a look into what their relationship is like.

"I do not ask for these only, but also for those who will believe in me through their word, that they may all be one just as you, Father, are in me, and I in you, that they also may be in us, so that the world may believe that you have sent me. The glory that you have given me I have given to them, that they may be one even as we are one, I in them and you in me, that they may become perfectly one, so that the world may know that you sent me and loved them even as you loved me." (John 17:20–23)

Jesus makes very radical claims here. First, He speaks to the God of Israel as "Father." This alone was blasphemous in the Jewish religious culture, for it was an indirect claim to be God's Son. Even more startling are His claims to oneness with the Father (see vv. 11, 21–22). Christ prays for the unity of His people, and the prototype is the oneness between the Father and the Son. This gets even more bewildering when a divine nature is also applied to the third person of the Godhead, the Holy Spirit (Matt. 28:19). This is eternal Trinitarian beauty. Barth got it right when he said, "The tri-unity of God is the secret of God's beauty. It is radiant and what it radiates is joy. It attracts and therefore it conquers. Once we deny God's threefoldness, we immediately are left with a lusterless and joyless . . . God."[2]

Let's trace the genealogy backward from created beauty to Trinitarian beauty using the example of color. Diversity of color is a source of great joy. A monochrome world is not quite as exciting as the colorful one we enjoy. The more color there is, the more diversity of visual beauty. From black-and-white to color TV, the revolution continued to high-definition color. My home HDTV brags of eight million individual pixels, each showing different colors at varying intensity—eight million dots of diversity yet unified in one screen.

Massive diversity in unity multiplies our pleasure. We celebrate it in everything: music (melody and harmony), architecture (forms and shapes in one "design"), athletic teamwork, and food (do I need to explain this one?). Even the mystery and pleasure of sexual union is a God-designed metaphor of plurality in unity.

Trinitarian metaphors go beyond the physical world to harmonies of relationship and truth. The greatest joys we experience in life are relational—family, marriage, friendship, and community. These strike us inwardly as being essentially good things that bring meaning to life in significant ways. We enjoy holidays (the coming together of the family), weddings and anniversaries (celebrations of the union of marriage), and Fourth of July parades (the unity of community and nation). Relational unity is humanity at its supreme and highest ideal. Think about your best memories. They probably have something to do with times of closeness with a parent, a child, a spouse, or a friend. Relational unity is beautiful because it whispers of the wondrous beauty of the Godhead's relational threeness and oneness.

THE SELF-GIVING GOD

We have finally come to the epicenter of all beauty. God's core is self-giving love (*agape*): the Father's love for the Son and the Spirit; the Son's love for the Spirit and the Father; the Spirit's love for the Father and the Son. Eternal, infinite, selfless love! Within the Trinity, the Father gives of Himself to the Son and the Spirit. The Son gives of Himself to the Father and the Spirit. The Spirit gives of Himself to the Father and the Son. The result of their eternal self-giving is eternal and perfect happiness within themselves. Their self-giving is beautiful both as an attribute of their nature and as a description of their relationships. True and essential beauty is love's joyous outflow of perfect, infinite, and eternal divine self-giving within the Trinity.

"The Father loves the Son and has given all things into his hand." (John 3:35)

Jesus said to them, "If God were your Father, you would love me, for I came from God and I am here. I came not of my own accord, but he sent me." (John 8:42)

"For this reason the Father loves me, because I lay down my life that I may take it up again." (John 10:17)

What do you notice in these verses? The Father loves the Son, and the Son loves the Father. How do they express this love to each other? Sending. Giving. Laying down. The Bible describes the essence of our God this way: "God is love" (1 John 4:8). Most people read that and think it describes how God relates to us— and that is gloriously true! More importantly, though, it describes how God relates to Himself and within Himself: perfect, selfless, joyous love.

So that we might know His love, God gave it expression in the drama of the incarnation and life of Jesus. Christ's earthly ministry was an unveiling of the inherent self-giving glory of the Son:

Have this mind among yourselves, which is yours in Christ Jesus, who, though he was in the form of God, did not count equality with God a thing to be grasped, but made himself nothing, taking the form of a servant, being born in the likeness of men. And being found in human form, he humbled himself by becoming obedient to the point of death, even death on a cross. (Phil. 2:5–8)

This famous passage is debated for what it says of Christ's nature. What is often missed is what it tells us about the Trinity's nature—specifically, the selflessness of divine love. He did not view His rights and privileges as the Son of God as glories for Him to self-manage. Instead, He relinquished them in obedience to the Father.[3]

In the mystery of eternity past, before the world's creation, God the Father made His will known to the Son. This plan included the creation of the world, the creation of man in His image, the fall of man, the role the Son would play in saving people from their sins, and His final return at the consummation of history. The Son willingly agreed. Why?

The essence of the Trinity is self-giving. Christ gave Himself over to the will of the Father. What was the Father's will? To display the glory of the self-giving Son to the Father and to display that glory to humanity as Servant and Savior. The Father's love motivates the unveiling of the Son's glory, and the Son's love motivates obedience to the Father. This divine summit of love is the source of all beauty everywhere. Jeremy Begbie helpfully points out,

As far as divine beauty is concerned, if the "measure" of beauty is outgoing love for the sake of the other, it will not be long before we are forced to come to terms with *excess or uncontainability*, the intratrinitarian life being one of a ceaseless overflow of self-giving. There is still proportion and integrity, but it is the proportion and integrity of abundant love.[4]

Do you see the great irony of the cross of Christ? The cross represents the most gruesome death man has ever devised. In the culture of its day, it was so profane that you would never talk about it in polite company. A cross would seem entirely out of place in a discussion of beauty. Yet the cross gives finite human beings a small taste of what it is like to be a member of the Trinity. In the moment of His sacrificial death, Jesus gave to us what He had given to the Father for all eternity: everything—the total surrender of self. The cross is love's highest human expression and beauty's ultimate declaration. Before a sunset, mountain range, painting, or song can be relished as beautiful, our souls must awaken to true beauty. The cross and resurrection of Jesus shine as supreme demonstrations of beauty. Everything else is a reflection.

THE GRANDEUR OF GOD'S GLORY

Like most pastors, I perform weddings—lots of them. If there is any compensation for the effort a wedding entails, it is the "moment" every pastor relishes. In a typical American wedding, the minister stands at the front of the church, with the view of views, as the bride makes her entrance. Over the years, I have learned to keep one eye on the bride and one eye on the groom. The look on his face is precious. He's dazed. He's befuddled. He's speechlessly experiencing something nearly transcendent, and his facial expression and eyes (and often beads of sweat) shout his wonder without him saying anything at all. It is the look of delight.

After doing weddings as a single pastor for many years, my day finally came. I would often joke I was always the minister, never the groom. My groom moment allowed me to feel what all those grooms I married off were experiencing. When the bride was my bride, and she came down the aisle to me, it was delight and

The greater the beauty, the higher the joy, and the higher the joy, the more it radiates outwardly.

wonder of the highest kind. I was the flabbergasted groom in the presence of stunning bridal beauty. And she was mine.

We might not suppose that delight would be so effusive. After all, we experience it every day. I sip my morning coffee. I enjoy it, but my facial expression hardly changes. I delight in my coffee on a certain level, but not on the bride-coming-down-the-aisle-toward-me level. Why? The greater the beauty, the higher the joy, and the higher the joy, the more it radiates outwardly.

These thoughts lead us to the subject of the glory of God. There is often confusion about this, as God's "glory" is mentioned in the Bible in two different ways. One is the worth or honor of God. We are to do everything "to the glory of God" (1 Cor. 10:31), and we are to "ascribe to the LORD glory and strength" (Ps. 29:1). In these and many other Scriptures, God's glory is revered and celebrated as His inherent worth and supremacy.

The other description of glory is its most dazzling and famous. The Bible records many sightings of the glory light. The most notable among them occurred one night on a mountain in Galilee. Jesus took Peter, James, and John and went up to a mountaintop, "and he [Jesus] was transfigured before them, and his face shone like the sun, and his clothes became white as light" (Matt. 17:2).

Can you imagine being there? Jesus lit up like a lighthouse. Two men appear with Him: Moses, representing the Old Testament law, and Elijah, preeminent among the prophets. The disciples, who were "heavy with sleep" (Luke 9:32), were now wide awake and filled with an adrenaline rush of terror.

What happens next truly terrorizes them. "[Peter] was still speaking when, behold, a bright cloud overshadowed them, and a voice from the cloud said, 'This is my beloved Son, with whom I am well pleased; listen to him.' When the disciples heard this, they fell on their faces and were terrified" (Matt. 17:5–6).

Notice two essential truths here. *Beloved* in the original language means "esteemed, dear, favorite."[5] It is an effective term of endearment and delight. *Well pleased* carries the meaning to enjoy or "take delight."[6] Put these two terms together, and we discover a divine truth about the relationship between the Father and the Son. Within the Trinity, there is a boundless and infinite delight in one another. What do we learn about the beauty of God here? Before you ever had a happy moment, or your great-grandparents had a happy moment, or Adam and Eve had a happy moment—before the universe was created—God the Father and God the Son and God the Spirit enjoyed a perfect and robust relational delight in one another. This inner-Trinity pleasure is God's most cherished beauty.

What the disciples saw was a fleeting unveiling of the glory of the second person of the Trinity. His glory was cloaked in a human body from the moment of conception in Mary's womb. This glory light had emanated from Him for all eternity past, but for these thirty years, it had remained hidden. On that mountain, for just a few moments, Jesus let some of it out. It was glory. Glory is the light of divine delight. Specifically, it is the brilliant, emanating overflow expression of God's infinite joy in being God. Glory light expresses God's glorious worth.[7]

God chooses to express His invisible, infinite worth in a visible, created way.[8] Glory to us looks like light. It is bright. It is radiant. But it is not light. It is like light, only whiter and purer. If we could capture a beam of glory light and put it under a microscope, we would discover that glory is much different than a sunbeam. A sunbeam carries within it the nature of the sun. Glory light carries the likeness of God Himself. It is a visible expression of the nature of God;

it is holy and spiritually intense. Its brilliance is described repeatedly in the Old Testament as "splendor" and "majesty" (1 Chron. 16:27; Pss. 21:5; 29:2; 96:6).

And there is remarkable consistency in the response of all who have seen it: terror and humility. Why? The glory of God is a visible display of the beauty and worth of who God is. It is the light of delight. It is what God's joy in Himself looks like when He allows us to see it.

That blessed and beautiful vision is what our souls crave. The outward joy of a groom for his bride portrays it. Our tears betray our longing for our own perfect experience of it. Some day we will see the reality. Then our suspicions will be confirmed: we were made for a more profound beauty, and the glorious vision of His beauty is the only experience that will satisfy the cravings of our soul.

Questions for Reflection and Discussion

1. Can you remember having a spontaneous encounter with beauty (like the story described at the airport)? What was it and why does it stand out in your memory?

2. How do you sense a craving for beauty within you?

3. Have you ever really considered the notion that God is beautiful? How might this way of thinking be new or different to you?

4. Take a few minutes to ponder the Trinity. Don't get frustrated or discouraged at the difficulty of understanding it fully in your mind—just let it produce a "wow" in your heart.

5. How do your closest human relationships (e.g., with a parent, spouse, children, friends) help you relate to the endearment and delight experienced between the members of the Trinity?

Chapter 2

The Beauty of Creation

Some years ago, a friend was house-sitting for a nationally famous Division I football coach while the team played in a bowl game. He invited me to hang out with him at the coach's mansion. I'll never forget the basement of this enormous house. It was filled floor to ceiling, including the support posts, with pictures of the coach with his teams, staff, and famous people such as US presidents and movie stars. I've never seen anything like it; hundreds of framed pictures of himself, each one meticulously set and mounted to impress any visitor with the importance of this coach.

While such a gaudy self-display may seem unbecoming for a mere mortal, it would be wrong for God not to delight in Himself. If we have eyes and ears to discern, the universe is a floor-to-ceiling photo montage of God's glory and grandeur.

HOW DOES CREATION "SPEAK"?

Scripture poetically and powerfully describes what created beauty's purpose is when it says,

> The heavens declare the glory of God,
>> and the sky above proclaims his handiwork.
> Day to day pours out speech,
>> and night to night reveals knowledge.
> There is no speech, nor are there words,
>> whose voice is not heard.
> Their voice goes out through all the earth,
>> and their words to the end of the world.
> (Ps. 19:1–4a)

The heavens declare the glory of God? I have watched many lovely sunsets, yet I have never heard them "say" anything audibly. Apparently, atmospheric speech comes in a different form. The rest of the passage unpacks the opening statement. The skies and the heavens proclaim a Creator ("the work of his hands"). The constancy of nature's speech is expressed in the consistency of the sky being over us. It is always there. It is always speaking. What the heavens declare is not limited by geography, time, or language. The summary statement is in verse 4: "Their voice goes out into all the earth, their words to the end of the world." Creation is constantly telling us something. Psalm 19 highlights the heavens with good reason. They are breathtaking.

If we have eyes and ears to discern, the universe is a floor-to-ceiling photo montage of God's glory and grandeur.

I am a sky gazer. At age twenty-two, I went on my first commercial flight. As we rose into the partly cloudy skies, I was giddy with excitement. I was astonished at seeing the blue-edged horizon glimpsed between the dancing wispy clouds. It was a vantage point on my world I had never seen before. It was stunning. Expansive. Imaginative. Colorful. Amazing.

While I have now flown more flights than I can remember, I still like the window seat. The sky says something soulish to me. Every society in human history has been fascinated with the galactic expanse above us. Some worship it, and some explore it. We all relish it.

Is "up" the only direction God's nature is expressed? Not according to Isaiah, who, as John 12:41 unveils, was given the marvelous privilege of seeing a vision of Jesus in heaven before His incarnation. Isaiah writes:

> In the year that King Uzziah died I saw the Lord sitting upon a throne, high and lifted up; and the train of his robe filled the temple. Above him stood the seraphim. Each had six wings: with two he covered his face, and with two he covered his feet, and with two he flew. And one called to another and said: "Holy, holy, holy is the LORD of hosts; the whole earth is full of his glory!" (Isa. 6:1–3)

The whole earth is full of His glory? Is the earth filled with the kind of glory light seen at Jesus' transfiguration? I have been to many places globally, but I have never seen divine glory light anywhere. Yet the angels cry out that the whole earth is full of His glory. In everything we see and smell and taste and touch in this world, there are reflections of the glorious character of God. The angels affirm what God Himself declared over His creation as He made it: it is good!

The Hebrew word for "good" in the creation account is *tob*. We might use "good" in the sense of "good job" or "good news." By this, we mean that something is favorable or pleasant. But "good" in Hebrew carries with it the sense of "beautiful."[1] That shapes the perception of what God is doing in Genesis 1 as He creates the universe. Six times God pauses to assess what He has made: light (1:4) is (beautifully) good, land and sea (1:10) are (beautifully) good, plant life (1:12) is (beautifully) good, ocean life and birds (1:21) are (beautifully) good, animal life (1:25) is (beautifully) good, all creation (1:31) is exceedingly beautiful.

Even God enjoys the created world. He looked at all He had made as an artist upon completing a masterpiece and exulted. "*Tob!*" Beautiful! He didn't merely evaluate the precision of His handiwork; He made an aesthetic assessment of it all. He declared that it was beautiful by His divine definition and delightful to His sensibilities. We are made in God's image. When something that God has made breaks in upon our senses, or when we see, hear, taste, or touch a God-made beauty, we also delight in its aesthetic goodness. From deep within us gushes forth a "*tob!*" Beautiful![2]

WHY IS CREATION BEAUTIFUL?

While some deconstruct all aesthetic assessments as culturally conditioned or mistake preference for biological necessity, the valid question is the relationship between God and creation. Is He in it? Above it? Beyond it? All worldviews strive to answer this. Jean-Paul Sartre, the famous atheist philosopher, insightfully noted that the fundamental philosophical problem is that something is there rather than nothing.[3] To his observation, I would add this question: Why is what is there so beautiful? If the mere existence of matter confounds us, explaining its universal symmetries and harmonies is baffling. Matter is a problem. Beauty is a marvel.

Why do many of nature's beauties have no utilitarian purpose except, it would seem, just to be? Did culture condition us to hear sound waves as perfect complements to each other, as in a simple chord? Is the brilliance of Bach or Beethoven a figment of our imagination? I like the admonition from Einstein, who apparently said about Bach, "listen, play, love, revere—and keep your trap shut!"[4] Might God say the same? Or are the sound waves we call music just a coincidence?

The worldviews of Eastern religions turn this truth inside out, not by denying creation's beauty but by worshiping it. What God made is so spectacular that humanity mistakes it for God. The naturalists hold beauty too low (uncreated), while the pantheists elevate created beauty too high (divine).

Christianity recognizes that the beauty of creation is a result of God's self-portrait. If creation's purpose is to resemble physically what He is like spiritually, what else could it be but astonishingly beautiful? The universe is not God, since God transcends what He has created, but it physically reflects His spiritual essence. God delights in parabolic revelations of who He is.

It is not vanity or narcissism for God to delight in images of Himself. God cannot sin, so He cannot place the highest worth on anything or anyone other than Himself. God is no idolator. Therefore, He must delight in His own glory and all created reflections of that same glory.

Like that football coach's basement, we live in the divine mansion filled with pictures of God. He created this galactic mirror so we can know Him. Creation reflects this with seeable, tasteable, touchable, hearable, and smellable reflections of His glory and beauty. This is what Isaiah heard the angels rejoicing. The whole earth is filled with His glory, and it is a "song about God."[5]

Paul sings God's song in Romans 11:36: "For from him and

through him and to him are all things. To him be glory forever. Amen." The prepositions in that verse summarize all reality; God is the source of all that is good and beautiful. He is also the One to whom they point and praise. As seventeenth-century Puritan theologian John Owen wrote,

> All goodness, grace, life, light, mercy, and power, which are the springs and causes of the new creation, are all originally in God, in the divine nature, and that infinitely and essentially. In them is God eternally or essentially glorious; and the whole design of the new creation was to manifest his glory in them by external communications of them, and from them.[6]

Creation speaks to us—every day, all the time, constantly shouting truths about spiritual reality. Did you hear it this morning as you got up? Did you feel any truth about God this morning as you took a hot shower? Did you taste any truth as you delighted in your morning coffee? Did you hear any divine reality as you heard a bird singing? Did you see any truth as you saw the blue of the sky? What have you felt, tasted, touched, seen, and heard today? The whole earth is filled with His glory. Everyday creation shouts to us: God is glorious! God is the Creator! God is a provider! God is love! God is there!

A BLIND EYE AND A DEAF EAR

Tragically, the vast majority of the eight billion people on earth began their day deaf and blind to the glory of God around them. They see and hear and eat and taste and touch, but they don't perceive God's glory through the delights surrounding them. Too often, we don't listen to it and, disastrously, don't perceive the truth our souls crave.

Theologians call God's communication through the created world the "natural revelation" of God. This is contrasted with what is called "special revelation," when God speaks in words (the Bible) or through Jesus (the incarnation). In both natural and special revelation, God is speaking to us. Accordingly, Francis Schaeffer titled his classic book *He Is There and He Is Not Silent*. We can rejoice that God has revealed Himself as a God who speaks to us and wants us to know Him. In natural revelation, God placed a portrait of Himself in everything He made: in the galaxies, the animals, the molecules, human relationships, sexuality, and everything else. Big and small, it all contains portraits of God.

Calvin insightfully writes, "There is certainly nothing so obscure or contemptible, even in the smallest corners of the earth, in which some marks of the power and wisdom of God may not be seen. . . . As soon as we acknowledge God to be the supreme Architect, who has erected the beauteous fabric of the universe, our minds must necessarily be ravished with wonder at his infinite goodness, wisdom, and power."[7] Elsewhere Calvin says, "There is not an atom of the world in which you cannot behold some brilliant sparks at least of his glory."[8]

It's exciting to consider, isn't it? Everywhere I look, everything I feel, hear, smell, and taste transmits the excellence of God through the beauty of creation. He is the beauty behind all beauty. This is the foundational truth that the apostle Paul lays for his magnum opus to the Romans. He begins his explanation of the gospel with man's inability to "hear" what creation is saying:

> For the wrath of God is revealed from heaven against all ungodliness and unrighteousness of men, who by their unrighteousness suppress the truth. For what can be known about God is plain to them, because God has shown it to them. For

his invisible attributes, namely, his eternal power and divine nature, have been clearly perceived, ever since the creation of the world, in the things that have been made. So they are without excuse. (Rom. 1:18–20)

Paul explains that God's invisible qualities are perceived through the things that have been made—specifically, His eternal power and divine nature. Both are "invisible," meaning they are spiritual realities, attributes hidden from us in the invisible, spiritual nature of God. Yet, as with the glory light, all of creation is a visible expression of the hidden nature of God. In other words, in creation, God chose to make spiritual reality visible in physical form. To put it another way, God created the universe to display His power. The scale and vastness of the universe are a revelation of God's immense power. Take a moment and consider how powerful God is if He created the universe out of nothing.

The size of the universe boggles the mind. In 2003, the Hubble Telescope set itself for the longest and deepest look into the universe in the history of astronomy. From September 24 through January 16, 2004, it performed nearly one million seconds of exposure. Researchers counted ten thousand galaxies in the frame. Doing the math, that same density across the whole sky area totaled two hundred billion observable galaxies (our Milky Way being just one of them). An average galaxy contains two hundred billion stars. The total number of stars in the observable universe is a staggering forty to fifty billion trillion. That's a number I can't begin to understand. A helpful illustration is that if each star were a dime, the pile of dimes would be as tall as a 110-story skyscraper and cover the entire North American continent.[9] Wow.

The universe is big. Why? To say something to us about the God who made it—He is bigger.

EVERYTHING IS THEOLOGY

It is much like the difference between the moon and the sun. Imagine you had never seen the sun; all you had was the moon. The moon would be thrilling. It is itself spherically beautiful as a perfect circle. It would be valued for lighting the earth. Its size would be admired as it is easily the most prominent light in the sky. People would be tempted to worship the moon, venerate it, or hallow it to provide the earth with the necessary light.

But if suddenly our sun appeared, the esteem for the moon would fall drastically. When compared to the sun, the moon is much less in every category. Should we realize that the moon reflects the sun's light, we would enjoy the moonlight for the sun's sake. It resembles the sun and reflects the sun without being the sun. It has its own aesthetical appeal and pleasure but no glory of its own. Its glory is its privilege to reflect the brilliance and grandeur of the sun.

Created beauties are all moonlight. Aesthetically pleasing and filled with pleasures and wonders. Yet, compared to the grandeur of their Source, they are merely reflective of His brilliance. This is what it means that the whole earth is filled with God's glory. This truth resounds in so much of Christian celebration and worship, including the following familiar hymn:

> *This is my Father's world.*
> *[And] to my listening ears*
> *All nature sings, and around me rings*
> *The music of the spheres.*
>
> *This is my Father's world.*
> *I rest me in the thought*
> *Of rocks and trees, of skies and seas,*
> *His hand the wonders wrought.*

This is my Father's world.
  The birds their carols raise,
The morning light, the lily white,
  Declare their Maker's praise.

This is my Father's world.
  He shines in all that's fair.
In the rustling grass I hear Him pass,
  He speaks to me everywhere.[10]

God communicates the whole of His essential beauty by creating a reflection of it. The reflection captures the essence without being the essence. Much like a mirror communicates an image without being the image itself, beauty communicates God without being God. It reflects His essential unity and harmony in forms our senses can take into our mind and soul. But it doesn't stop there. It can't. As Romans 11:36 states, all things are *from* God and *to* God. Beauty boomerangs from God into created beauty, then through the senses and soul of the image-bearer, and finally back to God with praise and glory.

The wonder of creation says so much, but it does not say enough. God tells about Himself in creation, but creation doesn't communicate how we can be saved from our sins. Paul tells us in Romans 1:20 that creation says enough for man to be held accountable to God. No one will be able to stand before God and say, "You didn't tell me about Yourself." God's response will likely be, "I spoke to you every day—you just weren't listening." As beautiful as creation is, it cannot tell us about Christ. It portrays a God, but not a Savior. Only the gospel of Jesus Christ can do that.

However, what creation does say is glorious and elicits questions that prime our hearts to receive Christ. Our hearts ask, *Who could do this? If God can do all of this, how wonderful and desirable* must He be? If God made me, wouldn't He care for me? The person who asks these questions is on the path toward the One to whom all beauty is intended to lead.

Since everything God created is theology, all creation is a treasure hunt in which God has left clues—essentially pictures of Himself. Each picture is de-

Beauty boomerangs from God into created beauty, then through the senses and soul of the image-bearer, and finally back to God with praise and glory.

signed to increase our desire for something more, for someone more. The beauties of this world whisper to our souls that there is Someone ultimate. But the ultimate is never found in the wonderland of creation. We keep looking and longing for the Beauty behind the beauty, the One who will satisfy the cravings of our soul. This explains why the drug addict keeps shooting up, the porn addict keeps looking, the materialist keeps buying, and the thrill-seeker keeps jumping. On the other side of one thrill is the constant need for another and a desire for something better.

C. S. Lewis wrote, "We are on the outside of the world, the wrong side of the door. We discern the freshness and purity of morning, but they do not make us fresh and pure. We cannot mingle with the splendours we see. But all the leaves of the New Testament are rustling with the rumour that it will not always be so. Some day, God willing, we shall get in."[11]

Why do we crave beauty? It is the moonbeam that can lead us to the sunlight.

Questions for Reflection and Discussion

1. Have you visited somewhere that especially impressed you? What did it say to you about God?

2. Do you have a favorite spot in nature that you visit regularly? If so, why?

3. Why is it important to distinguish that although God created nature, nature is not God?

4. The wonder of creation communicates to us real spiritual truth. But what are redemptive truths that nature alone is insufficient to communicate?

5. Do you agree that every human being bears more of a reflection of God than the rest of the universe combined? If this is true, what effect should it have on how you see yourself and others?

Chapter 3

The Beauty of Christ

One day, while on a walk, I happened upon a local politician. He began to fervently grumble about the state of things in our country and community. Perhaps he hoped my status as a pastor would help things improve. He listed grievance upon grievance, fear upon fear. I waited for him to pause to take a breath. When he did, I interjected, "It's almost as if the world needs a Savior." Knowing I am a pastor, he paused, smiled, and said, "Oh, that's good!"

As all our hopes in the latest technology or political messiah perpetually disappoint us, the longing remains for one in whom our hope can rest secure. We want someone we can look up to, believe in, and identify with. Image-bearers need a hero. More specifically, fallen humanity needs a Savior. All the longings of our hearts scream for just one beauty that restores, fulfills, and endures. Christianity heralds just such a beautiful one: Jesus Christ.

Remember my experience at Midway Airport? Stunning and brilliant musical beauty filled Concourse C, yet most travelers passed by without even noticing. This is a parable of the human dilemma. God has come and displayed true beauty to this world. Still, billions pass by and cannot hear or see what their hearts crave: transcendent, saving beauty. The apostle Paul writes:

> If our gospel is veiled, it is veiled only to those who are perishing. In their case the god of this world has blinded the minds of the unbelievers, to keep them from seeing the light of the gospel of the glory of Christ, who is the image of God. . . . For God, who said, "Let light shine out of darkness," has shone in our hearts to give the light of the knowledge of the glory of God in the face of Jesus Christ. (2 Cor. 4:3–6)

Satan is "the god of this world" who has blinded the minds of unbelievers from seeing the true glory of Christ. Christ is and always has been the glorious Son of God. We have already seen how His infinite worth expresses itself in glory light, as it did on the Mount of Transfiguration. His beauty is the measure of His desirability. Both are infinite. Because of spiritual blindness, however, His beauty and desirability are lost to the eyes of the unbelieving heart. They cannot "see" His glory nor wonder at His beauty. They don't see it, and they don't get it.

In verse 6, Paul describes what has to take place for the blinders of the heart to come off: "For God, who said, 'Let light shine out of darkness,' has shone in our hearts to give the light of the knowledge of the glory of God in the face of Jesus Christ." When God created the world, He spoke into the darkness and created light. Spiritually speaking, for a sinner to "see," God has to say within us, "Let there be light." We need light to see anything. Humanity needs the light of understanding to see the beauty that we long for.

Our search for meaning has been described as a blind man looking in a dark room for a black cat that isn't there. All the human-centered philosophies of this world fail precisely where we need them most to succeed. For us, this failure is devastating. Reflecting on her impending death, the French existentialist philosopher Simone de Beauvoir stated:

> I loathe the thought of annihilating myself quite as much now as I ever did. I think with sadness of all the books I've read, all the places I've seen, all the knowledge I've amassed and that will be no more. All the music, all the paintings, all the culture, so many places: and suddenly nothing. . . . Nothing will have taken place. I can still see the hedge of hazel trees flurried by the wind and the promises with which I fed my beating heart while I stood gazing at the gold mine at my feet: a whole life to live. The promises have all been kept. And yet, turning an incredulous gaze toward that young and credulous girl, I realize with stupor how much I was [cheated].[1]

Thomas Dubay comments on this: "For the thoughtful atheist death must loom as a crushing catastrophe. Everything good, noble, beautiful experienced throughout life is about to vanish, not simply for a week or two, not only for a century, but forever. On the atheist's premise death is a nightmare unbroken by a dawn."[2]

Blindness buries beauty. As atheist Bertrand Russell wrote, the sad result is life lived on "the firm foundation of unyielding despair."[3] This leaves us empty, living life—as T. S. Eliot poetically observed—as "hollow men."[4] What do we need? Light to see. When God shines this light into the darkness of human despair, something is perceived with the eyes of the heart. And that "something" is the glory and beauty of Jesus Christ.

THE BEAUTY OF CHRIST

Jesus is the Beautiful One, the most incredible beauty in all creation. His beauty is a tapestry of divine and human perfections harmonized in subtlety and majesty. This is one reason His beauty is missed; it is so different from anything we ever encounter. Jesus' beauty wasn't His physical appearance. By human standards, He didn't look like a Messiah. Isaiah 53:2 tells us that "he had no form or majesty that we should look at him, and no beauty that we should desire him." Significantly, the New Testament includes no description at all of Jesus' physical appearance. This is hard for Western culture to imagine because looks and appearance define our perspective of beauty and worth. When artists try to portray Jesus, He looks like the standard of beauty of each culture. He is depicted as white, black, brown, tall, short, muscular, thin, long-haired, short-haired, bearded, clean-shaven, and on and on. We want a good-looking Jesus, but for all the wrong reasons.

Jesus is a tapestry of all that is glorious in God intertwined with humanity's capability to reflect the image of God.

Scripture doesn't put a face on the Lord so that His true beauty can shine through. Jesus' beauty had nothing to do with His physical appearance. His was the arresting beauty of truth, purity, servanthood, passion, power, mercy, and love. Samuel Rutherford spoke of the loveliness of Christ, and Jonathan Edwards described His glory as the "admirable conjunction of diverse excellencies in Christ."[5] His beauty and His desirability were of a different—and more wonderful—kind. Jesus is a tapestry of all that is glorious in God intertwined with humanity's capability to reflect the image of God.

He Is Beautiful as the Perfect Image of God

Again, the apostle Paul says that when we are made alive to God, by God, we can see "the light of the gospel of the glory of Christ, who is the image of God" (2 Cor. 4:4). God is infinitely glorious and ultimately beautiful. Christ is the image of this beautiful God. Other Scriptures emphasize the same truth: "He is the image of the invisible God" (Col. 1:15). "He is the radiance of the glory of God and the exact imprint of his nature" (Heb. 1:3).

Humanity is made *in* the image of God; Christ *is* the image of God.[6] We resemble God's nature; Christ shares it. This is like the difference between seeing someone's picture and meeting them in person. A person is so much more than can ever be conveyed in a photograph. To meet the person is to see their nature, who they truly are. God loves pictures, and in this created wonderland, we are the high-definition pictures of God. Still, we are only pictures. Jesus is the exact representation of what God is like. "Whoever has seen me has seen the Father" (John 14:9).

Jesus doesn't show us what God is like by being similar to Him; He shows us what God is like by being the same as Him. Similar to how a sunray carries the essence of the sun, Christ is of the same essence as God. He is an extension of God's glory. He is the radiating glory through a human nature like ours.

The apostle John refers to Jesus as the one "which we have heard, which we have seen with our eyes, which we looked upon and have touched with our hands" (1 John 1:1). He "became flesh and dwelt among us, and we have seen his glory" (John 1:14). Jesus' glory shone through a normal human body to display His glorious deity. When we see and know and understand Him as Scripture reveals Him, we are seeing and knowing the essence of God's character.

Jesus' life expressed the infinitely beautiful God whose nature He shared.

Doesn't this explain the shocking nature of Jesus' life? God showed up on the earth, so it's no surprise that the world has never seen anything like the life and ministry of Jesus. Think of how the infinite and eternal love of God was experienced through Jesus' touch of the leper, how God's perfect mercy radiated through Jesus' response to the woman caught in adultery, how the glory of God's infinite power flashed as Jesus bid Lazarus back from the dead. Jesus' life expressed the infinitely beautiful God whose nature He shared.

He Is Beautiful in the Excellence of His Life

What is it about Jesus that captures people from all the cultures and religions of the world? I contend that it is His glory. Those closest to Him wrote of His majesty: "For we did not follow cleverly devised myths when we made known to you the power and coming of our Lord Jesus Christ, but we were eyewitnesses of his majesty" (2 Peter 1:16). "We have seen his glory, glory as of the only Son from the Father, full of grace and truth" (John 1:14). Is there any other person in human history who has the power of example that Jesus has? What other movement or religion or cause has a leader that can match up to Him?

Try to think of a moral or spiritual category in which He is not the highest expression ever. Think of His compassion, self-sacrifice, giving, love, and kindness. Think of an attribute that you wish was better represented in your life. Strength. Courage. Wisdom. Integrity. Leadership. Power. Humility. Jesus perfectly expresses it, doesn't He? He is the ultimate standard for every noble characteristic we admire.

R. E. O. White highlights Christ's character:

> His moral perfection lies in the unique balance of opposite virtues. It is the presence in one soul of seemingly contradictory qualities that gives his character its completeness; it is their perfect harmony that lends to His whole life that poise which is the perfection of strength. Strength of mind and will are so rarely wedded to gentleness; gentleness and sympathy do not always succeed in preserving the highest standards of righteousness and purity; and again righteousness and purity so rarely keep their tolerance and goodwill, especially towards the unrighteous and the impure. It seems enough if we could excel in one virtue or the other: Jesus reveals the summit of each one in symmetrical character.[7]

If Jesus isn't beautiful in our estimation, who or what is? What is He lacking? What could we want in a Savior that we don't find in Him? The human heart is blind to the Beautiful One while at the same time depressingly enamored with His pictures and reflections. Until the veil is removed, we can't "see" Him for who He is.

This is the wonder of salvation. Paul goes on to say that God "has shone in our hearts to give the light of the knowledge of the glory of God in the face of Jesus Christ" (2 Cor. 4:6). God's vehicle for this is the Holy Spirit, who makes us spiritually alive through regeneration by the power of the gospel. The result is that, for the first time, we can "see." John Newton wrote of this in his now-famous hymn, "Amazing Grace":

Wonder at His beauty leads to worship of His being.

"I once was lost, but now am found, was blind, but now I see." Our newly awakened spiritual vision allows us to see the glory of Jesus as Savior and Lord. We see His beauty, and we want Him.

Gospel wonder can save us when it convinces us that nothing is more desirable or beautiful than Christ. Once we are spiritually awake, we apprehend the beauty of Christ, and wonder grips our soul. As we have seen, wonder leads to worship. Wonder at His beauty leads to worship of His being. This is the death of the lie that something other than Christ can satisfy us—and the birth of new life in Christ. It is the restoration to what we were made for: wonder at and worship of the living Christ.

We Long for Him

We all crave perfect love. We desire the love of a mother, father, friend, or spouse. In the absence of love, we long for the love of anyone. We want enduring and unconditional love. Even the worst criminal locked up in prison longs for someone to love him. Have you ever thought about why? If the universe's origin is an accident, and if human beings are who they are through time and chance, why do all people want to be loved? Further, why are all human loves ultimately disappointing? No spouse loves us exactly as we want. Too often, family love erupts into friction and conflict. Friends fail us. We desperately want someone to love us perfectly.

As my friends and church family know, I spent many years as a single man. I lived alone for most of those until I was married at age forty-four. All those solo years gave me much time to reflect on the powerful longings in my heart: companionship and partnership in life, for a wife and children. There is a palatable ache within that can wash over you like waves of despair. I could analyze it. I could philosophize about it. I could even teach on it. But I could not overcome it. Even now, as a husband and father, I find these longings stalking me. Loneliness is one of humanity's most tender emotions. It reminds us that we are not made for ourselves. We were made for our Creator. The barbs of loneliness are God's way of saying, "Here I am!"

I came to discover that loneliness was not an enemy but a friend. When we wake up to the fact that no relationship can fully satisfy, we realize that we are lonely for God. Is this not what Jesus told the woman at the well? She thought she needed physical water, but Jesus knew what she truly longed for. It is the same thing you and I long for—Jesus. He is the One our souls crave. Jesus pointed out to her that everyone who drinks physical water will be thirsty again, but "whoever drinks of the water that I will give him will never be thirsty again" (John 4:14). The woman's response speaks for us all: "Sir, give me this water" (verse 15). Our thirsts show us what we need, and what we are thirsty for is Him. He is satisfyingly beautiful, and our desires reveal how much we miss Him and long for Him. This is the battle. As Dostoevsky points out, "The awful thing is that beauty is mysterious as well as terrible. God and the devil are fighting there and the battlefield is the heart of man."[8]

Who or what do we think is most desirable? Where does soul-satisfying relational beauty come from?

We think we want a spouse, but what we ultimately want is Him.

We think we want a friend, but what we ultimately want is Him.

We think we want a family, but what we ultimately want is Him.

We think we want anything, but what we ultimately want is Him.

He is the goal of our desires, and all the beauties of this world whisper His name. In the Chronicles of Narnia series, C. S. Lewis provides a picture of what it is like to come to see the beauty of Christ. Young Lucy sees Aslan, "the huge Lion, shining white in the moonlight."[9] She rushes to him and buries her face in his silky mane. Aslan rolls onto his side and Lucy lands softly between his paws. He bent forward and just touched her nose with his tongue. His warm breath came all around her. She gazed up into his large wise face.

"Welcome, child," he said.

"Aslan," said Lucy, "you're bigger."

"That is because you are older, little one," answered he.

"Not because you are?"

"I am not. But every year you grow, you will find me bigger."[10]

Jesus is bigger and more beautiful than our hearts can begin to imagine. God made every created beauty in this world as an expression of Christ's beauty and the beauty of the Father's love for the Son. Therefore, all beauty is a breadcrumb path that leads us to Christ.

Questions for Reflection and Discussion

1. Why is there a universal desire within mankind to identify with someone—some sort of hero or celebrity—whom we believe to be greater than us?

2. Why do you think Jesus is esteemed by people from every culture and religion of the world? But why, then, is He not embraced by more people as Savior and Lord?

3. In what ways can you relate to the claim that loneliness is not an enemy but a friend that communicates that the only relationship that can fully satisfy us is a relationship with God?

4. If you carefully consider it, how are your desires and the beauties of this world whispering Jesus' name?

Chapter 4

From Beauty to Wonder

A few years ago, I was blessed to go on a tour of the ministry of the apostle Paul in Greece. I had never been there and knew only a little about modern Greece. I have studied ancient Greece since my seminary days. Part of the tour was visiting some of the Greek islands. I knew very little of them since only a few appear in the biblical text. They announced our small cruise ship would be porting at the island of Santorini.

The tenders ferried us to shore, where we discovered we had to take a high lift to get up to the hotels and shops. Once we got to the top, my eyes beheld the most beautiful scenery I have ever seen. Santorini was an island volcano that erupted and then collapsed around the year 1600 BC. The devastating eruption left a rim of volcanic heights in a half-moon shape with a most glorious view. I was awestruck, along with everyone else. Very quickly, the cameras came out. The sun sets ideally over the caldera as providence would have it, only adding to the astonishing beauty.

When you see Santorini, get ready for a powerful inner emotion. What is this internal liveliness? Why is it there? Why do all humans experience it, long for it, and go to great lengths to see, taste, hear, touch, and smell anything that produces it within?

The answer is provided in the first chapter of the Bible. Humanity was bestowed a unique status that differentiates us from the rest of creation.

> Then God said, "Let us make man in our image, after our likeness. And let them have dominion over the fish of the sea and over the birds of the heavens and over the livestock and over all the earth and over every creeping thing that creeps on the earth."
>
> So God created man in his own image,
>   in the image of God he created him;
>   male and female he created them.
>
> And God blessed them. (Gen. 1:26–28)

Our status as image-bearers is the basis for man's inherent dignity, the equality of all humans, and the sacred value of all human life. These are all significant. What people miss is how our image-bearing relates to why we desire what we do. Our longings unveil our created purpose, and these correspond perfectly with the character of God. God is moral, spiritual, intelligent, communicative, relational, and personal. We are moral, spiritual, intelligent, communicative, relational, and personal. Is this a coincidence, or does it reveal our created purpose? When we consider the Bible's emphasis on the glorious beauty of God, what would we expect image-bearers of God to crave?

BEAUTY ADDICTS

The relishing of beauty is universal in all human cultures around the world. We cannot live without it. We are made in every way to delight in it. To see it. To hear it. To taste it. To touch it. To smell it. These senses enable us to receive into our minds and souls the world around us. It is no coincidence that we live in a cosmos filled with beautiful sights and tastes and smells and sounds, and we "happen" to have senses that correlate perfectly to them. Even without the biblical testimony, isn't it plausible that our capacities point to a Creator who made them for us and us for Him?

Isn't it plausible that our capacities point to a Creator who made them for us and us for Him?

Our desires also speak to our purpose. It all comes back to Genesis 1:26: "Let us make man in our image, after our likeness." We are made for God's beauty, and all beauty is God's beauty. When we see or hear or taste or smell one of the created reflections of God's beauty, we love it; something emotional and spiritual happens inside us.

THE WONDER OF IT ALL

Abraham Joshua Heschel was a Jewish philosopher who thought deeply on this subject. In the preface to one of his books, he wrote, "I did not ask for success; I asked for wonder."[1] Heschel adds this about wonder:

> The world of things we perceive is but a veil. Its flutter is music, its ornament science, but what it conceals is inscrutable. Its silence remains unbroken; no words can carry it away.... Awe

is a sense for the transcendence, for the reference everywhere to mystery beyond all things. It enables us to perceive in the world intimation of the divine . . . to sense the ultimate in the common and the simple; to feel in the rush of the passing the stillness of the eternal.[2]

His point is that wonder goes beyond words. We have already explored God as the Beauty behind all beauty. He created beauty in the universe to reflect what He is like. He gave us senses to see and hear and taste and smell, to experience created beauty. Beauty initiates in us an inward eruption. What was happening in me when I gazed at the caldera of Santorini? As an image-bearer, I was experiencing delight as a mysterious kind of bliss. This is wonder.

Wonder is what image-bearers feel when they glimpse a reflection of God's beauty. God has designed us in such a way that any experience of His glory powerfully moves us. And it is fantastic. Beauty brings us to tears, shouts, meditations, cheering, laughter, and sobbing. One writer described wonder's delight this way: "At such moments, one suddenly sees everything with new eyes; one feels on the brink of some great revelation. It is as if we caught a glimpse of some incredibly beautiful world that lies silently about us all the time."[3]

The fascination beauty creates does not terminate with the visual experience. It runs through our souls on a spiritual quest and hearkens a spiritual memory. The feeling turns theological deep within us.

BEAUTY: A GIFT AND A MAP

We must remember that we are living a story. At the beginning of the story (Gen. 2:8–12), we had it really good. We started in a garden. Every tree was beautiful to see and bore fruit that was delicious to eat. There were rivers, forests, gold, and precious stones. We were designed for garden living. Think of the most enjoyable place you have ever been. This garden was better!

Despite all the sensory beauty, the best part of it was that God was in the garden, and Adam and Eve were completely comfortable with Him. The last verse of Genesis 2 describes the vulnerability they enjoyed with God and one another: "And the man and his wife were both naked and were not ashamed" (Gen. 2:25). Everything was in perfect harmony: man and nature, man and wife, man and God. It was life as God intended. Embedded in our spiritual DNA is an ancient memory of when everything was as it ought to be. We retain this as a kind of spiritually suppressed memory. Beauty is beautiful to us when it includes harmony and balance. This can be relational harmony, color harmony, natural harmony, musical harmony, physical harmony, national harmony, and more. Beautiful harmonies are an echo in our hearts of ancient harmony, and we miss it. We want it again. That is why sensory beauty is not enough; we want to possess the beauty itself so the experience can continue.

This is beauty's blessing and curse. God created beauty for a purpose: to give us the experience of wonder. And wonder, in turn, is intended to lead us to the ultimate human expression and privilege: worship. Beauty is both a gift and a map. It is a gift to be enjoyed and a map to be followed back to the Source of the beauty with praise and thanksgiving. Adam and Eve did this with every experience of beauty in the garden. Every morning the heavens (and everything else) declared the glory of God, and as the first humans saw the

> **Beauty is a gift to be enjoyed and a map to be followed back to the Source of the beauty with praise and thanksgiving.**

sunrise, the beauty produced wonder, and the wonder led them
to worship. They saw the beauty all around them as a reflection of
God's nature and used it as a starting point to praise Him.

Wonder continues to offer us this starting point. As Robert
Fuller points out, "Wonder entices us to consider the reality of
the unseen, the existence of a more general order of existence
from which this world derives its meaning and purpose. It is thus
only to be expected that wonder also entices us to believe that our
supreme good lies in harmoniously adjusting ourselves thereto."[4]
To which pre-fall Adam and Eve would shout, Amen!

BEAUTY AND THE BEASTS

While the way life used to be sounds magnificent, something has
gone desperately wrong. We still love beauty, but it no longer leads
to its God-created purpose. What has happened? The apostle Paul
explains the devastating impact of sin on this natural progression
from beauty to worship:

> For although they knew God, they did not honor him as
> God or give thanks to him, but they became futile in their
> thinking, and their foolish hearts were darkened. Claiming to
> be wise, they became fools, and exchanged the glory of the
> immortal God for images resembling mortal man and birds
> and animals and creeping things. Therefore God gave them up
> in the lusts of their hearts to impurity, to the dishonoring of
> their bodies among themselves, because they exchanged the
> truth about God for a lie and worshiped and served the crea-
> ture rather than the Creator, who is blessed forever! Amen.
> (Rom. 1:19–25)

Sin distorted everything, including creation's harmonies and their purposes within us. Beauty's purpose is to lead us to worship God, but verse 21 says, "For although they knew God, they did not honor him as God or give thanks to him." Created beauty should lead us to give God honor and thanks. Giving Him honor means to esteem Him highly or to adore Him. Giving Him thanks means acknowledging that God is the source and Giver of all that is good (James 1:17). We are made in such a way that "the things that have been made" (Rom. 1:20) ought to generate adoration for the Creator and gratitude for His generosity to us. Worship is wonder's appointed goal.

So why is it that people experience wonder, but they don't worship? The fall from created perfection to sinful imperfection has darkened our understanding, and our thinking has become futile (Eph. 4:17–18). The result is that we are confused about where to place the glory. Beauty still creates wonder, and wonder still searches for someone to give praise for the beauty. However, without God, we are left to worship the beauty for its own sake. We worship created things rather than the Creator (Rom. 1:25). Our wonder collapses onto itself, leaving us to worship stuff and matter. This is the bane and emptiness of our materialistic secular age. Image-bearers designed for a life of meaning lived in a relationship with God are emptied of significance by bowing to an "it." The only way an image-bearer of God could descend to such an inane level is for a lie to be mistaken for the truth (Rom. 1:25). This is what has happened, and is happening, all over the world.

THE LIE: SOMETHING ELSE IS MORE
WONDER-FILLED THAN GOD

We are duped into believing that there is something better than God. This deception has taken place on such a universal scale that it seems normal. He who is infinitely beautiful is set aside, and the fleeting goosebump is treasured. How can this be? Sin comes with a set of blinders, so we cannot see what is actually beautiful, desirable, and spiritually satisfying. "The god of this world has blinded the minds of the unbelievers, to keep them from seeing the light of the gospel of the glory of Christ, who is the image of God" (2 Cor. 4:4). What is the result? Image-bearers gasp at the Grand Canyon, clap at concerts, wait in line at the art museum, line the beach for sunsets, crowd their favorite restaurants, admire the wealthy, and on and on it goes. When it is done, what are we left with? Ecclesiastes repeats a haunting human experience—meaninglessness. Emptiness is what image-bearers feel when they worship beauty for its own sake.

That is the futility and madness—there is no experience of beauty in this world that lasts. Sunsets fade. Food rots. Vacations end. Music stops. There is not a single wonder-producing created beauty in this world that endures. Our world in general, and human beings in particular, are like grass. "And all its beauty is like the flower of the field" that "withers" and "fades" (Isa. 40:6–7). Everything here is so despairingly fleeting. The despair of our Western culture is that we have the most pleasures and the least satisfaction. We have the most stuff, and we are still not happy. Doesn't it feel like something in life is missing?

We can look to our culture's heroes for examples of this. Every year there are a few shocking celebrity deaths that create brief searches for meaning among their fans. After one high-profile example, a writer expressed his bewilderment that this actor should die of a prescription drug overdose. He wrote, "It's hard for the average movie fan, including yours truly, to totally grasp why a guy like Heath Ledger—drop-dead handsome, popular, incredibly talented—could be depressed about anything."[5] It's hard to grasp if you think image-bearers of God could ever find meaning in good looks and fame. But clearly, those things are not enough for an image-bearer of God. We are made for God, and all our wonder moments are a search for Him. Sin is us looking for meaning in all the wrong places. Reflections of God in creation create wonder, but not the satisfaction we truly want.

Blaise Pascal insightfully puts it,

There once was in man a true happiness of which there now remain to him only the marked and empty trace, which he in vain tries to fill from all his surroundings, seeking from things absent the help he does not obtain in things present. But these are all inadequate, because the infinite abyss can only be filled by an infinite and immutable object, that is to say, only by God himself.[6]

Even before Pascal, about 1,600 years ago, Augustine thought deeply about these things and said, "You have made us for yourself, and our heart is restless until it rests in you."[7]

Millenniums come, and millenniums go. Our quest for one perfect beauty and ultimate wonder continues.

Questions for Reflection and Discussion

1. In the words of the ancient theologian Augustine, to what extent is your restless heart finding its rest in God? How can you increase your satisfaction and rest in Him?

2. Describe a wonderful moment from your childhood. What factors contributed both to the experience and lasting memory of it?

3. What is one of your favorite vacation destinations? How does that place satisfy a longing within you to experience beauty?

4. Reflect on a time in your past when you subtly believed the lie that a created thing would bring you long-lasting happiness.

5. Pick a recent moment of wonder. How might you respond differently now that you have read this chapter?

Chapter 5

From Wonder
to Worship

Let's do a quick review. God is triune, and His three-in-oneness is the absolute beauty of all. God's beauty summarizes all His excellencies and perfections; in particular, each member's self-giving for the joy of the others and the harmony of the whole. Jesus is the most precise expression of God's glory and beauty in physical form. God created the world to unveil the glory of the Son and engineered the universe to reflect physically what He is like spiritually. We are the pinnacle of creation and uniquely designed to respond with joy and wonder when our senses interact with reflective divine beauty. We call that wonder and pleasure. It happens naturally, by design.

But what next? Is this all about goosebumps and inner emotions? How does a Christian live spiritually alive in the aesthetically pleasing world around us? Two centuries ago, a poor Methodist woman wrote of a simple but happy day in her life:

> I do not know when I have had happier times in my soul than when I have been sitting at work with nothing before me but a candle and a white cloth, and hearing no sound but the sound of my own breath, with God in my soul and heaven in my eye. I rejoice in being exactly what I am—a creature capable of loving God and who, as long as God lives, must be happy. I get up and look for a while out of the window and gaze at the moon and stars, the work of an Almighty Hand. I think of the grandeur of the universe, and then sit down, and think myself one of the happiest beings in it.[1]

This woman knew a secret, an ancient truth long forgotten by most. Beauty leads us to wonder. Wonder finds its prescribed consummation in the worship of God.

OF CLOUDS AND HORSES

It is a self-evident truth—when you love something, you love everything that reminds you of it. There is no end to the pleasure this produces. My daughter loves horses. She reads books about them. She dreams about them. She chooses movies about them. She is horse crazy. We were staring at the sky one day, and I said, "What do the shape of those clouds remind you of?" Any guess? She said, "Horses!" Her love for horses causes her to see them everywhere she looks.

One of the sure signs that a couple is falling in love is they take pictures. Why do lovers cherish photographs of their beloved? In reality, the image is not the person. It is a piece of paper with colored dots or a combination of pixels on a screen. Its significance comes from its resemblance. When you love someone, you treasure everything that reminds you of them.

The experience of salvation is like that. It is transformational. When God turns the light on in our soul through the gospel, we perceive a greater glory than anything in this world. We perceive the glory of Christ and the majesty of His death and resurrection. We recognize it spiritually, by faith, and a dramatic inward transformation occurs by the Holy Spirit.

Paul wrote about this. "These things God has revealed to us through the Spirit. . . . The natural person does not accept the things of the Spirit of God, for they are folly to him, and he is not able to understand them because they are spiritually discerned" (1 Cor. 2:10, 14). The "natural person" refers to human beings in a state of spiritual deadness. The gospel often seems like nonsense to them. What is going on within is deeply theological, though the "natural person" cannot sense it. What must happen to fix this? The Spirit of God must reveal the glory of God in Christ to the mind and heart, or there is no understanding.

Without Christ, God's glory, beauty, and desirability are lost on us. Wonderfully, the reverse is also true. When I am made spiritually alive, I see truth that I could not and did not see before. I used to worship a thing and think it was God. Now I am enabled to love and cherish the one true God as Creator and see everything as a reflection of Him.

LOVE THE MOON FOR THE SUN'S SAKE

Returning to our illustration of the sun and the moon—if all you had ever seen was a full moon, you might think it was the sun. After all, there are remarkable similarities. A full moon is big and bright. Imagine what it would be like to see the sun in all its brilliance for the first time. The moon would be usurped in your estimation by something more magnificently brilliant and beautiful. You would never look at the moon the same way again. There would still be much to enjoy about moonlight, but it would be appreciated for what it is—a reflected light.

Every created pleasure and beauty that we have ever desired in this world is like moonlight. Void of any enhanced comparison, they seem like the best this life has to offer. But through the gospel and the Holy Spirit, we have seen the radiant glory of the Beautiful One, Christ.

This changes our perspective on the pleasure of moonlight beauty. We used to worship reflections, but we discern a better beauty through the gospel and the Holy Spirit. Until we see the beauty of Christ, we will never see the true beauty in anything else. Once we discern His glory, however, we enjoy created beauties all the more because they remind us of Him.

We enjoy the moon because we love the sun. Jesus is the person we love. The created world is the reflection. If we love Him, we will love every resemblance and see everything good and true in the universe as a portrait of Him. This is a Spirit-enabled perspective that turns wonder's sensory experience of beauty into an occasion for joy, reflection, and worship.

TRANSPOSING WONDER INTO WORSHIP

The Holy Spirit restores our created capacity for wonder-inducing worship, yet we can still experience wonder without worship. I know. For many years, although I was a Christian, I walked beaches, viewed sunsets, enjoyed music, watched movies, ate desserts, and stared at the stars pretty much like an atheist. I enjoyed these things immensely, but primarily for their own sake and for the sensory pleasures that accompanied them. Based on my conversations with other Christians about this subject, my story is all too familiar. We have largely missed out on pleasure's ultimate high and God's intended purpose for it.

The reasons for this are many, but the chief culprit is pride. Romans 1:20 says God's purpose in creation is to display His character. Because of our pride, however, we remain deaf and blind. We presumptuously accept the joys and pleasures of God's creation without giving His purposes proper consideration. "Although they knew God, they did not honor him as God or give thanks to him, but they became futile in their thinking, and their foolish hearts were darkened" (Rom. 1:21).

Paul describes how sin has incapacitated image-bearers from responding rightly to created beauty. He says we "did not honor him as God or give thanks to him." Hearing what we have failed to do also tells us what we are supposed to do. We were made to respond to created beauty in two ways: giving God honor and giving God thanks.

GIVE GOD HONOR

The meaning of the Greek word for honor is "to render or esteem glorious."[2] To honor something or someone means to magnify its value. The heavens are declaring the glory of God by magnifying the glory of their Creator (Ps. 19:1). The whole earth is resplendent with God's glory (Isa. 6:3). Every created thing is declaring the truth about God and giving honor to Him. Image-bearers participate in this praise by contemplating the glory of God in our moments of wonder. To give God honor is to agree with what the experience of beauty is intended for.

This is challenging because it is not readily apparent what a flower or mountain, for instance, is saying about God. Flowers and mountains allow us to think about God and marvel at His creativity and power in creating the thing itself. The lesser beauty leads to contemplations of the greater. At least it should, though this doesn't happen automatically. The Spirit is available to help us discern the greater beauty, yet our minds and hearts must be trained to consider it. Loving God motivates active contemplation of the wonders around us.

As the psalmist writes, "On the glorious splendor of your majesty, and on your wondrous works, I will meditate" (Ps. 145:5). This is the power and blessing of beauty. Ugliness doesn't stir the heart toward God. Ugliness doesn't resemble Him at all. Beauty creates delight in us and arouses spiritual affections. Wonder-producing beauty is an opportunity for us as Christians to consider the glory of the One who created it in the first place. All beauty whispers to us in this way. These are calls to worship, going from what I can see, hear, smell, taste, or touch to what I cannot. My thoughts go from the visible to the invisible, from the created thing to the Creator. When my wonder gets me there, I esteem Him as glorious by giving God honor for both the beauty and my enjoyment of it. Having seen the sun (Jesus), the Christian relishes the wonderful experience of the moon (earthly beauties) as a sublime reflection of His beauty and maximizes the pleasure by offering God praise.

GIVE GOD THANKS

We all have those happy providences when something unexpectedly good happens to us. Have you ever put your hands in a pocket and discovered a long forgotten $20 bill? These occasions make us cheerful inside, and we can't wait to tell someone about our good fortune. What is often lost on us at these times is the responsibility to thank God as the Giver of all good gifts. Thanklessness was on display when Jesus healed ten lepers, but only one came back to thank Him (Luke 17:11–19). Jesus poignantly asked, "Where are the other nine?" Giving thanks honors the generosity of the giver. It acknowledges that I am the recipient of a gift and honors the person who gave it.

Paul describes false teachers as those who deny the goodness of God's created gifts to us: They "forbid marriage and require abstinence from foods that God created to be received with thanksgiving by those who believe and know the truth. For everything created by God is good, and nothing is to be rejected if it is received with thanksgiving" (1 Tim. 4:3–4). What do we have that we have not received from God? When we experience a moment of beauty, we should turn wonder into worship by giving thanks to God for His goodness in providing it, for His creativity in making it, or simply for our pleasure in experiencing it. Consider this famous verse: "Whether you eat or drink, or whatever you do, do all to the glory of God" (1 Cor. 10:31). When I'm with friends and say the prayer before a meal, I occasionally include these words: "Help us eat this meal like Christians." After the amen, an exciting discussion usually ensues about what it means to eat like a Christian.

Eating is an excellent example since we all do this multiple times a day. For Christians, a meal can and ought to be a worship service. Some eating experiences are potentially more worshipful than others. Peas are more challenging to turn into worship than, let's say, strawberry pie (a favorite of mine). How does one eat strawberry pie like a Christian? A slow-motion, frame-by-frame replay of a bite of strawberry pie sends joyous anticipation to my heart. As the fork places the pie on my palate, taste buds start dancing in my mouth. The flavor of strawberry sweetness sends a sensation from my tongue to a pleasure zone in my mind. As I chew, the flavor is distributed throughout my mouth, and its sweetness creates further delight. Of course, one bite is not enough. I begin the process all over again—savory bite after savory bite—until, sadly, the whole piece of pie is gone.

Strawberry pie and other delicacies are eaten around the world every day. Yet if I simply eat and enjoy them for their own sake without thought of God as the Creator and Giver of the pleasure, then I am eating strawberry pie like an atheist. My wonder and delight are experienced for their own sake. In other words, when we fail to acknowledge God as both the Giver of the pleasure and the Beauty behind the beauty, we are missing beauty's intended purpose—to lead us to Him.

The key is to love God in such a way that we actively contemplate God's goodness in the granting of pleasure or wonder. Doing this with thanksgiving is what Psalm 145:5 calls us to do: "On the glorious splendor of your majesty, and on your wondrous works, I will meditate." We give God honor when we give Him thanks and acknowledge Him as the giver of all good gifts, whether big or small.

Questions for Reflection and Discussion

1. Beauty can bring us to tears, cheers, meditation, laughter . . . which best describes your typical response?

2. What thoughts and feelings do you have when you reflect on the garden of Eden as Adam and Eve experienced it?

3. Can you relate to the observation that embedded in our spiritual DNA is an ancient memory of when everything was in harmony as God intended it to be? How so?

4. When have you felt the emptiness that comes from worshiping beauty for its own sake? Or to put it another way, when have you felt the despair, pervasive in our Western culture, of having the most pleasures and the least satisfaction?

Chapter 6

Enjoying God in What He Makes

As I write this, there is an immersive art exhibit near me in Chicago. It features the art of Vincent van Gogh. It is immersive by using projectors displaying a singular masterpiece on the floor, ceiling, and walls of a room. Not only do you see the work of genius, but it envelopes you on every side. They market this as "don't just see the art, feel the art." The experience allows the art lover to do what art lovers have longed to do since paint and canvas first started dancing together. You can step into the art to be part of it. The upward and side glances give the sense of not just seeing but experiencing. Even van Gogh may have wished to walk, look, and breathe in his own art.

We live every day in the immersive art exhibit of God. It is below us, around us, above us, and beyond us. As we have seen, God placed it where it is and made it as it is to immerse us in His goodness and glory. In salvation, the ancient eyes of our soul have opened afresh to this radiant divine splendor. Yet, like every spiritual exercise, we can grow in our aesthetical doxology as we train our senses to turn wonder to worship.

HE SHINES IN ALL THAT'S FAIR

As I mentioned earlier, everywhere my horse-loving daughter looks, she sees a horse. Everywhere a Christian looks in creation, we see a reflective fragment of the God we love. As Calvin pointed out, every atom of this world contains sparks of God's glory. We must consciously look for these "sparks" all around us, for as the hymn writer said, "He shines in all that's fair."[1] To go beyond created beauty to God's beauty, we must perceive the reflections of God's beauty in the world around us. To perceive it, we must be looking for it. Looking for it requires a kind of spiritual discernment enabled by the Holy Spirit and empowered by our love for God.

This is seen in the life of Jonathan Edwards. He kept a journal that he called "Shadows of Divine Things," where he would record observations of the beauty he observed in nature. He and his wife, Sarah, enjoyed discussing these "shadows" because they saw them as the "language of God." Edwards describes his growing enjoyment of God in the beauty around him:

> After this my sense of divine things gradually increased, and became more and more lively, and had more of that inward sweetness. The appearance of everything was altered: there seemed to be, as it were, a calm, sweet cast, or appearance of divine glory, in almost everything. God's excellency, his wisdom, purity, and love, seemed to appear in everything; in the sun, moon, and stars; in the clouds, and blue sky; in the grass, flowers, trees; in the water, and all nature.[2]

Once our heart is alive to God's beauty in Christ, it is also alive to God's beauty everywhere else. Our eyes must search for what our spiritually alive hearts delight in—anything that reflects God's beauty. In our fallen world, the beauty of God is obscured by creation's brokenness and our visual impairment. Mike Mason illustrates this challenge nicely: "If I'm looking for a perfectly clear crystal stone on a beach, I may not find one, but if I look for the crystalline in stones, I'll see it gleaming everywhere."[3] God gleams from every molecule and atom of this universe. He is the beauty within and beyond every wonder-creating sensory experience. As we delight in God, our senses search for opportunities to enjoy Him in the lovely sights, sounds, smells, tastes, and textures all around us.

The opportunity to perceive God in beauty goes beyond created beauties to include character qualities in people that mirror God Himself. God's character is seen to an extent in all image-bearers, but it should be most evident in the transforming effects of the gospel in Christians. God is conforming us to the image of His Son (Rom. 8:29).

An ancient writer urges, "Every time you feel in God's creatures something pleasing and attractive, do not let your attention be arrested by them alone, but passing by them, transfer your thought to God and say: 'O my God, if Thy creations are so full of beauty, delight and joy, how infinitely more full of beauty, delight and joy are Thou Thyself, Creator of all!'"[4] As the beauty of Christ's character is revealed in us, the Christian community gives us ample opportunities to enjoy the qualities of Christ we see in others.

SWIM UPSTREAM

Beauty whispers to our soul the truth about God. How do we discern what that truth is? First of all, it requires a good understanding of who God is, as revealed in Scripture. It isn't easy to see how a picture looks like someone if you don't know what they look like in the first place. When you know and love someone, however, you can see their resemblance in the picture. It then becomes meaningful to you. You love the person, so you love anything that reminds you of them. Knowledge of the more precise image of God from Scripture and through the life of His Son dramatically helps us see His reflected portrait in creation.

Ever since the fall, our thoughts naturally flow in one direction: from the beauty to our enjoyment of it. Sin tilts created beauty toward us. But this is not beauty's designed purpose. Since created beauty speaks of God, our experience of it requires us to swim upstream. Beauty's glory and satisfaction are found in the source, not the self. We must do what is counterintuitive to the sinner; in the wonder of beauty, we must think backward.[5]

We should consider what this sensory pleasure might communicate regarding what God is like during our moments of wonder. This requires that we relate the experience to what we know about God. If the object of beauty is big, think of the vastness of God. If it feels soft, think of the tenderness of God. If it is simply appealing somehow, think of how great God must be since He is infinitely more desirable than the pleasure it provides. Perhaps it is merely inward amazement that asks, *Wow, how did He do that?* Relate it to God, and in so doing, turn the pleasure into praise. Wonder animates our spiritual senses, which can guide upward and Godward.

This is how we give God both honor and thanks and enjoy the wonder of His glory. To this, John Piper writes:

> We don't just stand outside and analyze the natural world as a beam [of sunlight], but let the beam fall on the eyes of our heart, so that we see the source of the beauty—the original

Beauty, God himself. . . . All of God's creation becomes a beam to be "looked along" or a sound to be "heard along" or a fragrance to be "smelled along" or a flavor to be "tasted along" or a touch to be "felt along." All our senses become partners with the eyes of the heart in perceiving the glory of God through the physical world.[6]

A soulish partnership is the spiritual function of our five senses—to "become partners with the eyes of the heart in perceiving the glory of God." For this partnership to be successful, we must actively contemplate God in the experience and direct our wonder toward Him in worship. Clyde Kilby was a man who understood this. He wrote a list of personal resolutions to help him stay alive to the beauty of God's world around him.[7] Among them are:

- At least once every day I shall look steadily up at the sky and remember that I, a consciousness with a conscience, am on a planet traveling in space with wonderfully mysterious things above and about me.

- I shall open my eyes and ears. Once every day I shall simply stare at a tree, a flower, a cloud, or a person. I shall not then be concerned at all to ask what they are, but simply be glad that they are. I shall joyfully allow them the mystery of what Lewis calls their "divine, magical, terrifying, and ecstatic" existence.

- I shall sometimes look back at the freshness of vision I had in childhood and try, at least for a little while, to be, in the words of Lewis Carroll, the "child of the pure unclouded brow, and dreaming eyes of wonder."

Kilby resolved to do these things because beauty becomes familiar and easily taken for granted in the daily routines of life. I did part of my schooling in Phoenix, Arizona. Being from the flat Midwest, I was fascinated by the rugged appearance of Phoenix's Camelback Mountain. I drove by it every day. The first week I stared in awe. The second week I looked at it. The third week I noticed it. I was driving by it by the fourth week, like all the other Phoenicians, mostly oblivious. Beauty is all around us. We see it, hear it, feel it, smell it, and taste it every day. Yet, do we *really* perceive the glory of it all? A life of wonder requires childlike fascination at the simple pleasures of everyday life.

I am challenged by these words from Thomas Dubay: "Wonder at reality demands the humility to sit at the foot of a dandelion. The proud are so full of themselves that there is little room to marvel at anything else."[8] Or Pond's pithy statement, "If we are too big for little things, we are too little for big things."[9] Our pride gets in the way of enjoying God and His good gifts! I watch my young daughters play. They are completely without regard for what others might think of their silliness. There is little egotism, and therefore, no fear of peer ridicule or adult displeasure. This frees them to enjoy fully what they are enjoying presently. I watch them with envy. My adult perspective is too guarded and, unfortunately, too restricted. I don't have as much fun as they do because my adult self has lost permission to adulate with reckless abandon. Only the humble will marvel at the dandelion.

Take a moment and think of all the beauties and pleasures you have already experienced today. What did you do with them? Where did your thoughts take you? Did you give honor and thanks to God? Or has the wonder of a sunrise, a child's hug, the smell of brewing coffee, a hot shower, birds chirping, a gentle breeze, highway wildflowers, or an image-bearer in the mirror been missed?

ENTHUSIASTICALLY ENJOY
THE CREATED BEAUTY ITSELF

While God's primary purpose in beauty is to draw our hearts to Him, that isn't the only purpose. In God's common grace to humanity, He intends for His creation to be enjoyed and relished. The Preacher in Ecclesiastes exhorts us:

> Go, eat your bread with joy, and drink your wine with a merry heart, for God has already approved what you do.
> Let your garments be always white. Let not oil be lacking on your head.
> Enjoy life with the wife whom you love, all the days of your vain life that he has given you under the sun, because that is your portion in life and in your toil at which you toil under the sun. (Eccl. 9:7–9)

The apostle Paul supplements that by describing God as the one "who richly provides us with everything to enjoy" (1 Tim. 6:17). While these experiences should draw our thoughts to God, they will also maximize our enjoyment of the created beauty itself.

C. S. Lewis meditated on this principle in terms of first and second things:

> The woman who makes a dog the centre of her life loses, in the end, not only her human usefulness and dignity but even the proper pleasure of dog-keeping. The man who makes alcohol his chief good loses not only his job but his palate and all power of enjoying the earlier (and only pleasurable) levels of intoxication. . . . Every preference of a small good to a great, or partial good to a total good, involves the loss of the small or partial good for which the sacrifice is made. . . . You can't get

second things by putting them first. You get second things only by putting first things first.[10]

Christians who properly place God as the source and goal of the things they enjoy will find themselves enjoying those things even more. In this, a Christian's experience of beauty should be a kind of apologetic for the gospel.

In truth, the way Christians relish created beauties ought to outstrip that of unbelievers since we neither find our identity in them nor hold on to them as ultimate. What if Christianity was known for creating higher and better experiences of pleasure? It is a gospel shame that Western Christians are known for the opposite. In part, I write this book to change that perception. If the secular world thought their enjoyment of music, drink, sex, friendship, art, and everything else was second-rate, might they look at Christianity and the gospel with keener interest?

Keeping aesthetical pleasure as a means instead of a goal is counterintuitive to our natural desire for more and more of a great experience. However, when we enjoy something for God's sake, it balances this obsessive tendency, and we are free to enjoy our pleasures wholly and openly. A Christian's God-focused enjoyment of creation makes it taste better, look better, feel better, smell better, and sound better. While turning beauty into worship is a divinely ordained human responsibility, it is no mere duty. Several years ago, I spoke to my church a message titled "Sex to the Glory of God." I discussed with my congregation that sexual intimacy should be a regular occasion for married couples to give God praise. Have you considered why God made sex pleasurable for us? He could have made it merely instinctual like it is for all the other mammals. But for us, He gave it a wondrous delight. Needless to say, I had a captive audience for that message.

Sometime after that, a retired couple in our church bought a new home and then had me over for dinner to show me their new place. After a lovely meal, it was time for the tour. The wife showed me the family room, the kitchen, the finished basement. Throughout the home, I saw pictures of their kids and grandkids on the walls. It was all very standard stuff. Then she took me down the hallway of bedrooms, finishing at the master bedroom. Here she opened the door and said with a smirk, "And this is the worship center!" I looked at her dumbfounded, and then I realized what she was saying! Beyond a bit of embarrassment, I admired what it said about both their relationship with one another and their relationship with God.

Sex in marriage is good and right and holy. It produces wonder, which is an opportunity for a Christian to turn it into praise. Sexual pleasure doesn't require breaking out into the "Hallelujah Chorus," but it does require giving God honor and thanks for all His good and beautiful gifts. The overarching theme of this book is that every room, every place, everything God provides is an opportunity to worship Him "who richly provides us with everything to enjoy" (1 Tim. 6:17).

Consider these words of a familiar Christian hymn from the perspective of beauty, wonder, and worship:

O Lord my God, when I in awesome wonder
Consider all the worlds Thy hands have made.
I see the stars, I hear the rolling thunder,
Thy pow'r throughout the universe displayed.

Then sings my soul, my Savior God to Thee;
How great Thou art, how great Thou art!
Then sings my soul, my Savior God to Thee;
How great Thou art, how great Thou art![11]

God's created beauties lead to wonder in the heart of an image-bearer. We can't help it. Turning the wonder toward God in worship fulfills the created purpose of both the beauty and the beholder of the beauty.

Questions for Reflection and Discussion

1. Can you relate to the experience of staring in awe to obliviously driving by Phoenix's Camelback Mountain? What do your experiences tell you about created beauty's diminishing returns?

2. How does being spiritually alive enable Christians to see things, particularly truths about God, they could not and did not see before?

3. Do you sometimes find yourself enjoying created beauties and pleasures immensely—but "like an atheist"? How can you fight against the temptation to do so?

4. Summarize in your own words what it means for us to "think backward" in regard to the wonder of beauty? Why is doing so counterintuitive for us?

5. How have you perceived God-like beauty in the character qualities of fellow image-bearers? Is it sometimes difficult for you to see that beauty? Why or why not?

6. What do you think of the assertion that a believer eating a meal can and should be a "worship service"? How does this assertion challenge your traditional thinking about such things?

7. Name one common activity of life that you will more consciously approach as an opportunity to give God honor and thanks. How can you stay focused in your attempts to do so?

Chapter 7

Enjoying God in What We Make

E ach weekend at my church, children do what van Gogh did; they draw things. Sometimes they give their creations to me. I ask them who the Martian-looking figure is. Often, they say, "It's you, Pastor Steve!" My daughters regularly create art for me as well. It is one of the true joys of being a dad. The problem is they make so much we have to dispose of them discreetly. If they spot any of their art in the garbage, they protest like we are throwing away the *Mona Lisa*.

The difference between the children's art and van Gogh's painting is around $50 million. Why did Vincent van Gogh paint? Why do our children draw? For similar reasons, the Egyptians built the pyramids, the Aztecs built their temples, and an Indian emperor built the Taj Mahal. Modern people paint their homes, do their hair, wash their cars, write poems to their lovers, and take family pictures. We are passionate about expressing ourselves in every sensory category. Like God-made beauty, man-made creations of beauty also move us profoundly. The cultures of history's civilizations are primarily defined by how their people expressed themselves in artistic expressions such as architecture, music, dance, pottery, and clothing. From the beginning, humanity has made beautiful things. Our culture today is dominated by artistic expression and our passion for it. The digital age has brought art to our fingertips. Art from all around the world and from every era of history is accessible for viewing, downloading, or purchase. It is so common that we can easily miss the weighty reasons we love both our creations and the beautiful creations of fellow image-bearers who are gifted to create.

WHY WE LONG TO CREATE

Answering why we love to create beauty requires another look back to our origin to see where this creative impulse comes from. Genesis 1 gives us the creation narrative and includes God's blueprint for the human race: "God created man in his own image, in the image of God he created him; male and female he created them" (Gen. 1:27). As we have already seen, bearing the image of God means that we, like God, have an aesthetic appreciation for beauty. This goes much further than merely appreciating beauty, however. God has built into our DNA a version of His imagination and creative expression.

God's creation was and is fundamentally different than ours in that God created everything out of nothing. Our creations are more of a creative rearranging of raw materials that God has made.[1] The painter uses God's colors. The dancer uses a body God designed. A musician borrows God's sound waves. Only God has ever created something out of nothing. Serious consideration of what that means is one more reason to be in awe of Him.

Yet humans also create. We can imagine something and then take it from a mental concept to actual reality. Our first glimpse of human creativity is Genesis 2:19: "Now the LORD God had formed out of the ground all the wild animals and all the birds in the sky. He brought them to the man to see what he would name them; and whatever the man called each living creature, that was its name" (NIV). What is more natural for a human than to name something? Even a little child will name her blanket or doll.

There are billions of life forms on our planet, yet only humans name things. Where does that impulse come from? It comes from somewhere deep within us: *our imagination*. Humans uniquely have imagination. To imagine something is to create it mentally and conceptually. We do this every day and don't think anything of it. We imagine the day ahead of us. We imagine what we will wear. We imagine the route we will drive to work. We imagine conversations we will have. We imagine potential solutions for issues we face. Our minds can conceive of things in potentiality before we make them reality. Even reading this page and allowing small shapes to represent words that correspond to concepts requires symbolic representation that soars beyond any other creature.

Our imaginative ability is fascinating. If we are simply a biological mass of evolved molecules, how can we create something in our mind before we do it? There is no naturalistic explanation for human imagination. But the Christian worldview has an explanation: we do because God did. God imagined the world before He made it. He contemplated making man before He did it (Gen. 1:26). Creativity begins in the imagination. God gave that ability to us. Adam saw the animals, and from within him came a creative impulse to make verbal representations of what he saw: giraffe, frog, leopard, Eve.

As a result of the fall, man lost his innocence, but not his creative ability. Over time this ability expressed itself in organizational and artistic ways. The Bible credits Jubal with the discovery and development of instruments and music (Gen. 4:20). Then Tubal-Cain began making tools, and humanity's culture launched into creatively shaping the human environment to meet human needs (Gen. 4:22). It's important to realize that from the beginning, humankind created things that weren't just utilitarian but were crafted artistically, in the same way the Creator made a blue sky and a green tree and a red robin. The Bible celebrates artists such as Bezalel (tabernacle), David (songwriter), and the musicians playing music in temple worship. Jesus was an artisan, and the son of an artisan, who learned his trade from His builder father. God likes it when image-bearers reflect His character by creating beauty. The divine Artisan made us little artisans, and beauty has been a considerable part of our lives and culture ever since.

WHAT IS GOD'S KIND OF ART?

Rather than saying that art needs to be overtly "Christian" or deal with religious themes to be appropriately enjoyed, we need to view all art through a biblical worldview. From this perspective, everything is speaking theologically. That is what God's kind of art does; it proclaims what is true about God. While creation is fallen, the universe of God's art celebrates what is true about God. However, in a fallen world, all human art speaks with oscillating contradictions and inconsistencies. Even the natural world groans with sin-created tensions between life and beauty, on the one hand, and death and decay on the other. It anticipates when everything it says and does is true once again (Rom. 8:19–23).

Man's artful expressions are also self-contradictory. We are not what we were made for, and our art is not what it could be. As Pablo Picasso famously said, "Art is a lie that makes us realize the truth."[2] Human minds spiritually darkened by the effects of sin often worship created things rather than their Creator (Rom. 1:25). Their lifestyles will show a desperate search for meaning, and their songs, poems, and sculptures will too. Human imagination creates perspectives on reality that express the hopelessness and emptiness of bearing His image but not knowing Him.[3]

This, too, is very theological. To the Christian mind, matured to see the world through the grid of the biblical story, these expressions can create wonder at human achievement without glorying in the worldview it communicates. Rather than saying that some art is secular and some art is sacred, we do better to view everything as sacred or sacredly defined. The impulse to do so is from God. The incarnation of imagination into art is also God-like. All human expression speaks of God, either in consistencies or in contradictions, and the Christian mind searches for and delights in every truthful resemblance of God. From the Christian worldview, all art is like that. It all speaks of what is sacred, and everything communicates either truth or falsehood. Truth is beautiful, and error is ugly. If there were nothing beautiful, there would be nothing ugly.

The ultimate example of this is hell itself, even as it breaks our hearts to consider it. Hell speaks the truth of God's love and beauty by displaying how ugly its absence is. When art is anti-God, the Christian worldview stretches to see it for what it is—a lie—and to view the lie as an opportunity to glory in the beauty of truth. Ugliness helps make the excellent and beautiful more desirable.

Experiencing human art is at times uplifting and redemptive; often, it magnifies what is corrupt, fallen, and flowing from man's lower nature. The challenge for us is that we inevitably experience both in the course of man-made beauty. So what is God's kind of beauty? Remember, like a yardstick is a yard and measures a yard, God is beauty and measures all beauty. The degree to which human beauty expresses God's beauty is the degree to which God delights in it (and so should we).

This is why God the Father rejoices over Jesus: "This is my beloved Son, with whom I am well pleased." Jesus is the exact representation of God's being, the perfect mirror eternally showing who is the fairest of them all. God's kind of beauty is His beauty. The world, the Word, and His Son are the only perfect reflections. Our artistic expressions and interpretations lack clarity and precision since we only see His beauty "like puzzling reflections in a mirror" (1 Cor. 13:12 NLT).

Yet we can express and appreciate what we know about God. Beautiful art will reflect the excellence, goodness, harmonies, virtue, and redemptive glory of God. In this, beauty is in the eye of the beholder as long as we recognize God as the Beholder of all beauty. It is our privilege to join with God's delight in man-made beauty's splendor and reflected theological brilliance.

The challenge comes when the beauty is enjoyed for its own sake. The wonder leads to worship of the artist, the music, or the emotional experience instead of God. As C. S. Lewis said, "The unbeliever is always apt to make a kind of religion of his aesthetic experiences."[4] He must do so because beauty enriches life and temporarily masks the pain.

Some years ago, I was blessed to walk through the Sistine Chapel and view Michelangelo's masterpiece on the ceiling. He painted it in the early 1500s, and it is considered one of the most outstanding examples of human artistry. If the heavens declare the glory of God, looking up in the chapel declares the glory of Michelangelo. The authorities require silence in the chapel, but ironically, the security guards shushing to keep people quiet amplifies the noise and clamor. This illustrates the experience of human art. While it can be astonishingly beautiful, there's always brokenness in the experience of it. Our wonder has to survive the shushing guards of a fallen Eden.

A Christian is free to relish the wonder that music or any other beauty creates within as long as it doesn't stop there. Just like the sunset or the mountain view, these moments of wonder and joy must be turned into Godward worship (giving Him honor and thanks), or we are merely experiencing man-made beauty as any atheist can.

A Christian's experience of wonder and joy in beauty should be far greater than that of a non-Christian. What is religious ecstasy to an unbeliever is just the beginning of wonder's blessing for a Christian. The unbeliever has nowhere to go with his experience and is left to crave it again. Go to another concert. Have another sexual encounter. Watch the same movie over and over. The Christian takes the wonder and uses it to animate praise to God. This consummates our joy in the beauty and glorifies God as the Giver of beauty's blessings. In this way, we enjoy man-made artistic beauty for what God intended it to be—a wonder-producing, praise-inducing experience of His glory.

ALL BEAUTY IS GOD'S BEAUTY

Like God-made beauty, man-made beauty requires us to bring God into the enjoyable sensory experience by relating it to what we know about Him. For example, the apostle Paul read the Greek poet Aratus's *Phaenomonea* and saw the truth that "we are indeed his [God's] offspring," and quoted Aratus to the Athenians at Mars Hill (Acts 17:28). We can do the same with our modern-day poets, singers, painters, and all the rest. We can mine for truth in the art and turn it into worship. Most often, this calls us simply to rejoice with thanksgiving that God has blessed us with the experience of beauty (1 Thess. 5:18). Every good thing comes from God (James 1:17). The ability of the artist is a gift from God. The art itself is a gift from God. The happiness I feel in the art is a gift from God.

Let me illustrate with my most fantastic experience of manmade beauty. A group from our church went on a tour of Israel. Our travels took us through Italy, which allowed me and a couple of friends to spend a few days in Rome. One day we heard that the city of Rome would be celebrating the conclusion of Advent with a performance of Handel's *Messiah* at the famous Basilica di Santa Maria Maggiore. The concert was free and open to the public. No question about it—we had to go. We arrived thirty minutes early and found the cavernous church packed. Romans love beauty. Yankee ingenuity got us some seats.

As we waited for the concert to begin, I looked at the people around me. It was a slice of the Roman population: young and old, rich and poor, cultured and common. All were drawn to hear Handel's brilliance and the skill with which Italian artists could express it. As the symphony began and the music cascaded off the cathedral's soaring ceilings, something happened inside me. My heart started a slow eruption. It is hard to even now to put it into words.

When the famed "Hallelujah Chorus" began, I was alive with the beauty of it. My soul was dancing with a long-dead composer. Together we were celebrating the wonder of Christ. It was a duet—image-bearer and image-bearer—Handel and me. One was the creator of the beauty and the other the beholder of it. My mind went from Handel's brilliance to thanksgiving to God for the sheer joy I felt.

If musical beauty can do this inside of us, what must the Creator of it be like?

All great art will contain an echo of Eden.

This is how human art can lead to worshipful contemplations about the ultimate Beauty. Artists can be worship leaders if we let them. We must let their art lead us to God through the consistencies or contradictions between their artisanry and the truth of the redemptive story God has written for all of human history. All great art will contain an echo of Eden: Eden in its original glory, Eden that is lost to us, and Eden restored. Christians who know and love God's redemptive story will spot this storyline and rejoice in it. This allows us to both critique and enjoy the artistic beauty we make. Both are critical. Analysis without enjoyment misses out on what God has made us for. Pleasure without discernment makes us susceptible to the negative value system often portrayed in a fallen world by fallen artists describing their perspective on reality. The former miss out on the fun, while the latter risks folly. God wants us to enjoy all beauty as His beauty and for His sake.

Questions for Reflection and Discussion

1. Have you ever thought about how amazing and powerful human imagination is (i.e., the ability to create something in our minds before we actually do it)? What would happen if we suddenly lost this capacity?

2. Since God is the divine Artisan who made us to be little artisans, how could you better use the creative imagination that He gave you?

3. How would you answer the question of whether there is such a thing as "Christian" art, music, etc.?

4. What do you think of this statement: "Hell speaks the truth of God's love and beauty by displaying how ugly its absence is"? How might hell's absence of anything beautiful shape your view of eternity?

5. Do you feel that Christians experience the joy and wonder of beauty to a greater extent than non-Christians do? How might this opportunity to maximize wonder and worship motivate you in the future?

6. What are the most significant ways this book has challenged you to enjoy God in everything?

Conclusion

A s our exploration of pleasure and joy in God comes to an end, let's review our thoughts on beauty thus far. The foundation of it all is that God is Himself the ultimate Beauty. The triune God is beautiful and is the most desirable reality in all that is. We are made in His image, we are made for Him, and we crave His beauty. He is the goal and satisfaction of all our desires, and all the created beauties of this world hint at His infinite beauty. As image-bearers, whenever we experience beauty, we can't help but feel delighted in it. The joy that beauty produces is wonder. God intends for us to turn that wonder toward Him in worship by giving Him honor and thanks.

Before the fall, Adam and Eve did that perfectly in every aesthetic joy—they did everything "to the glory of God." But after the fall, beauty is enjoyed by humans purely for its own sake. We worship created things rather than our Creator. Our culture lives for weekends, vacations, sports, sex, money, food, music, the Oscars, and much more. We are utterly frustrated that these things produce no lasting satisfaction, and we cannot understand why.

By the power of the gospel, God takes the blinders off so we can see what our souls crave: God and His glory incarnated in the person and work of Jesus Christ. He begins to restore this image of God in us. Now we begin to see things differently. We start seeing the imprint of God in the world around us. The heavens declare the glory of God, and everything else does too. We begin to enjoy life for God's sake. Everything is a theological springboard because all of it relates to God as Creator and Redeemer. Now we can see the sunset and hear it shouting the glory of God. We can look at a monarch butterfly and once again see and sense the amazing Creator. The perception of God is restored in all beauty because it all speaks of Him. This includes beauties that fellow image-bearers create. Dance and music and photography and interior decorating and cinema and sculptures are opportunities for beauty to lead to wonder and for wonder to lead to worship.

UNBEARABLY BEAUTIFUL

I was talking with a lawyer friend of mine who surprised me with a comment he made as he explained a favorite song. He described the music as "unbearably beautiful." The more beautiful something is, the more frustration we feel as we contemplate it. No matter how beautiful something is, our joy in it ebbs. Wonder never lasts. The concert ends. The sun sets. The feast is eaten. The thrill that beauty gives us soon disappears. And then what are we left with? Craving for more. This is the law of diminishing returns. The more we see, taste, hear, touch, or feel something, the less joy we derive from it. Buy that favorite song, and after hearing it a hundred times, it's not our favorite anymore. Buy a giant chocolate chip cookie at the mall, and the last bite isn't as good as the first.

Have you seen a current picture of _____ lately (fill in the blank with any movie star from thirty years or more ago)? Today's starlets are tomorrow's yawns. Proverbs says it with haunting wisdom: "Charm is deceptive, and beauty is fleeting" (Prov. 31:30 NIV). As God's Word tells us, "The world is passing away along with its desires" (1 John 2:17). We need a new world where beauty never fades, and the wonder of it never goes away.

ALL THINGS ALWAYS NEW

The apostle John was given a vision of the future. The future for God's people is a new heaven, a new earth, and a new city. John begins his description in this way:

> Then I saw a new heaven and a new earth, for the first heaven and the first earth had passed away, and the sea was no more. And I saw the holy city, new Jerusalem, coming down out of heaven from God, prepared as a bride adorned for her husband. And I heard a loud voice from the throne saying, "Behold, the dwelling place of God is with man. He will dwell with them, and they will be his people, and God himself will be with them as their God. He will wipe away every tear from their eyes, and death shall be no more, neither shall there be mourning, nor crying, nor pain anymore, for the former things have passed away." (Rev. 21:1–4)

Doesn't this sound fantastic? We were made for this place and for this kind of experience with God. The relational language is so intimate. He will dwell with us. We will be identified as His people, even as His bride. He will deal personally with us, wiping away our tears.

Let's consider those tears for a moment. Apparently, in eternity our tear ducts will be operational. I have generally taken this to refer to tears of sadness or suffering. That may be. However, we don't just cry when we're sad—we also cry when we're overjoyed. What kind of tears will be wiped from our eyes? When we step into our eternal home, and our feeble understanding of God's infinite goodness begins to dawn on us, we will gaze with wide eyes and dropped jaws at the beauty of our new home. As we start to experience, spiritually and physically, the presence of God with us, we will understand with glorified minds His infinite love for us. As these dawn upon our comprehension, we will look around and see, hear, smell, taste, and touch the fresh splendors of our new home. Then it will dawn on us that this glorious experience will never end, and we will weep happy tears that our God will tenderly wipe away. Could it get any better?

In the final book of the Chronicles of Narnia series, the Unicorn says it well when he arrives in the "new Narnia": "I have come home at last! This is my real country! I belong here. This is the land I have been looking for all my life, though I never knew it 'til now. The reason why we loved the old Narnia is that it sometimes looked a little like this one."[1]

Just think—if this world's pleasures are so breathtaking, how wonderful must the real thing be? Only then will we do rightly what we are learning to do now (and what this book is all about). Our happiness in eternal beauty will quickly take our thoughts and worship to God. The beauty will remind us of Him, teach us about Him, give us occasion to meditate on what is true about Him. What requires intentional backward thinking in this world will be as natural as breathing in the next.

Will we remember what delighted us in this world? Certainly, but it will be different. As we see, hear, feel, taste, and smell in eternity, we will often say, "Do you remember _____ (insert any earthly beauty)?" Eternal beauty will remind us of this world's wonders and pleasures, but only faintly. We won't miss them or long for them. Why would we? We will finally be where all is right, and nothing could be better.

This book's purpose is to walk with you toward what you truly want. Ultimately, that is not the experience of beautiful music or beautiful food or beautiful fragrances or beautiful stories or beautiful homes or beautiful bodies or perfect friendship or blissful marriage or any love or pleasure this world has to offer. We were made for a better place and a better person, and all the beauties of this world whisper that to our soul. We crave Christ. He has made this restoration possible and offers Himself to humanity as Savior, Redeemer, and Restorer. The end of the Big Story is beautiful because the end of the story is God. This world and its histories are prelude and foretaste; all the sunrises and sunsets, symphonies and rock concerts, feasts, and friendships are but whispers. They are a prologue to the grander story and an even better place. Only there, it will never end. J. I. Packer said it so well: "Hearts on earth say in the course of a joyful experience, 'I don't want this ever to end.' But it invariably does. The hearts in heaven say, 'I want this to go on forever.' And it will. There can be no better news than this."[2]

When we see infinite beauty, the absurdity of living for the fleeting pleasures of what this world has to offer will shock us. Only then will we begin to apprehend the real purpose for this wonderland.

I have two young daughters. Over these precious early years, I view coming home from the office as typically the highlight of the day. "Daddy!" They rush at me with screams and giggles. After hugs and kisses, they often say, "Daddy, let's play!" I say, "What do you want to play?" One of their favorites is hide and seek. I say,

"You girls hide, and I'll count to ten." Off they skip to hide in their favorite spots. "1, 2, 3 . . . 10! Ready or not, here I come! Where are those girls!" I hardly start looking when I hear from under the ottoman, "We're over here!" They cannot help themselves. Why do they give away their tactical position? It is simple—because they want to be found.

Why did God make the galaxies? The color spectrum? Music? Image-bearers with fantastic creativity? He wants to be found. He wants you to find Him. Everything beautiful in the cosmos whispers His presence. Still, nothing says it with the power and clarity of the incarnate, beautiful Jesus and the trillions of created reflections of His infinite glory. Like a breadcrumb trail, earthly beauty chaperones us on a path to "see" the beauty of Christ, for His beauty to lead to wonder, and for wonder to lead us to a life of worship.

Acknowledgments

This book urges wonder and thanksgiving to God. I happily apply these to this page of appreciation.

Thank you to my beautiful church, Bethel Church. You are such a lovely expression of a gospel-formed community. I am most grateful to the elders, pastors, and leaders whose support on this project made such a difference. I love you and thank you!

Thank you to the great publishing team at Moody Publishers. Thank you to each who worked personally on this project and Trillia Newbell in particular. Your enthusiasm for this book moved it from an idea to reality. Thank you!

This book adapts much from my longer previous book on this subject, *Eyes Wide Open*. The strong reception of that book was thanks to many; Tim Beals and Credo, Tim Challies, Tony Reinke and Desiring God, Phil Ryken, Leland Ryken, Sam Storms, and others. Thank you to each; your advocacy continues to bear fruit in this second volume.

Thank you, Brad Lagos, for your role in the questions for discussion and reflection. Your keen eye and mind made both books better.

I also thank ministry friends whose past and present friendships have played a role in this publication. You know who you are! Of special note are my dear friends Wilbur and Ardelia Williams, whose passing this year accentuates our mutual love and my indebtedness to you.

My faith was nurtured in a home where the kingdom of God was first and foremost. Thank you, Mom and Dad, for introducing me to Jesus. Thank you to Barb, Scott, and Teri for special years together on Northview Drive.

Finally, a very special thank you to my lovely wife, Jennifer, and my daughters, Kiralee and Madeline. Other than Christ's love, the love I enjoy with you is the greatest I have ever known. Thank you for bringing beauty into every day we have together. Let's make all things beautiful and enjoy God forever. I love you . . . so much!

Notes

INTRODUCTION

1. C. S. Lewis, *Till We Have Faces: A Myth Retold* (London: Harcourt, 1984), 75.
2. John Calvin, *Institutes of Christian Religion* (1536), 4th ed. (Kissimmee, FL: Signalman Publishing, 2008), loc. 1011.
3. Cornelius Plantinga Jr., *Engaging God's World* (Grand Rapids: Eerdmans, 2002), 6.
4. Hugh Evan Hopkins, *Charles Simeon of Cambridge* (Grand Rapids: Eerdmans, 1977), 203.

CHAPTER 1: THE BEAUTY OF GOD

1. Jonathan Edwards, *The Nature of True Virtue: A Jonathan Edwards Reader*, ed. John E. Smith, Harr S. Stout, and Kenneth P. Minkema (London: Yale University Press, 1995), 252–53.
2. Karl Barth, quoted by Belden C. Lane in *Ravished by Beauty: The Surprising Legacy of Reformed Spirituality* (Oxford: Oxford University Press, 2011), 159.

3. I read this term ("relinquished") applied to Philippians 2 many years ago.

4. Jeremy S. Begbie, "Created Beauty: The Witness of J. S. Bach," in *The Beauty of God: Theology and the Arts*, ed. Daniel J. Treier, Mark Husbands, and Roger Lundin (Downers Grove, IL: InterVarsity, 2007), 29.

5. Carl Grimm, *A Greek-English Lexicon of the New Testament*, trans. Joseph Thayer (New York: Harper & Brothers, 1887), 4.

6. Rick Brannan, *The Lexham Analytical Lexicon to the Greek New Testament* (Bellingham, WA: Lexham Press, 2011), Logos Bible Software.

7. "The glory of the Lord, therefore, is the supereminently luminous beauty of divinity beyond all experience and all descriptions, all categories, a beauty before which all earthly splendors, marvelous as they are, pale into insignificance." Thomas Dubay, *The Evidential Power of Beauty: Science and Theology Meet* (San Francisco: Ignatius Press, 1999), 45.

8. Jonathan Edwards describes the glory of God as "fitly compared to an effulgence or emanation of light from a luminary, by which this glory of God is abundantly represented in Scripture. Light is the external expression, exhibition and manifestation of the excellency of the luminary, of the sun for instance: it is the abundant, extensive emanation and communication of the fullness of the sun to innumerable beings that partake of it. Tis by this that the sun itself is seen, and his glory beheld, and all other things discovered: it is by a participation of this communication from the sun, that surrounding objects receive all their luster, beauty, and brightness." Jonathan Edwards, *The Works of Jonathan Edwards*, vol. 1 (Carlisle, PA: The Banner of Truth Trust, 1995), 119.

CHAPTER 2: THE BEAUTY OF CREATION

1. James Swanson, *A Dictionary of Biblical Languages with Semantic Domains: Hebrew (Old Testament)*, 2nd ed. (Oak Harbor, WA: Logos Research Systems, Inc., 2001), entry 3201.

2. "A beautiful thing involves no good except itself, in its totality as it appears to us. We are drawn towards it without knowing what to ask of it. It offers us its own existence. We do not desire anything else, we possess it, and yet we still desire something. We do not in the least know what it is. We want to get behind beauty, but it is only a surface. It is like a mirror that sends us back our own desire for goodness. It is a sphinx, an enigma, a mystery which is painfully tantalizing. We should like to feed upon

it but it is merely something to look at, it appears only from a certain distance. The great trouble in human life is that looking and eating are two different operations. Only beyond the sky, in the country inhabited by God, are they one and the same operation." Simone Weil, quoted in Richard Harries, *Art and the Beauty of God: A Christian Understanding* (New York: Continuum, 2005), 95.

3. Francis A. Schaeffer, *He Is There and He Is Not Silent* (Carol Stream, IL: Tyndale, 1972), 1.

4. Albert Einstein, quoted in *Forms of Performance: From J.S. Bach to M. Alunno (1972–)*, ed. Michael Maul and Alberto Nones (Wilmington, DE: Vernon Press, 2020), 16.

5. Thomas Dubay, *The Evidential Power of Beauty: Science and Theology Meet* (San Francisco: Ignatius Press, 1999), 321.

6. John Owen, *Meditations on the Glory of Christ* (Ross-shire, Scotland: Christian Focus Publications, 2004), 150.

7. John Calvin, *Calvin's Commentaries*, vol. 4 (Grand Rapids: Baker, 1993), 308–9.

8. John Calvin, *Institutes of the Christian Religion*, trans. John Allen (Philadelphia: Presbyterian Board of Publication, 1843), 58.

9. Hugh Ross, *Why the Universe Is the Way It Is* (Grand Rapids: Baker, 2008), 31.

10. Maltbie Babcock, "My Father's World," in *Thoughts for Every-Day Living* (New York: Charles Scribner's Sons, 1901), 180.

11. C. S. Lewis, *The Weight of Glory* (New York: HarperCollins, 1980), 43.

CHAPTER 3: THE BEAUTY OF CHRIST

1. Simone de Beauvoir, *The Force of Circumstance*, cited by Joseph Ratzinger in *Faith and Culture* (Chicago: Franciscan Herald Press, 1971), 45; quoted in Thomas Dubay, *The Evidential Power of Beauty: Science and Theology Meet* (San Francisco: Ignatius Press, 1999), 99.

2. Dubay, *The Evidential Power of Beauty*, 99.

3. Bertrand Russell, *A Free Man's Worship: The Basic Writings of Bertrand Russell* (New York: Simon and Schuster, 1961), 67.

4. T. S. Eliot, "The Hollow Men" (1925), in *Poems 1909–1925* (London: Faber and Faber Limited, 1934), 123.

5. Jonathan Edwards, *The Excellency of Christ*, sermon preached at Northampton (Boston: Thomas Dicey, 1780), 10.

6. I read this somewhere many years ago during an expositional series through the book of Hebrews.

7. R. E. O. White, *Into the Same Image: Expository Studies of the Christian Ideal* (London: Marshall, Morgan & Scott, 1957), ch. 11, and 158; quoted in R. E. O. White, *Christian Ethics* (Herefordshire, UK: Gracewing, 1994), 122. Augustine was so captured by Jesus' beauty that he wrote a song about it: "He was beautiful in heaven, then, and beautiful on earth: beautiful in the womb, and beautiful in his parents' arms. He was beautiful in his miracles but just as beautiful under the scourges, beautiful as he invited us to life, but beautiful too in not shrinking from death, beautiful in laying down his life and beautiful in taking it up again, beautiful on the cross, beautiful in the tomb, and beautiful in heaven. Listen to this song to further your understanding and do not allow the weakness of his flesh to blind you to the splendor of his beauty." Augustine, *The Works of Saint Augustine: Expositions on the Psalms*, vol. 3 (Hyde Park, NY: New City Press, 2000), 283.

8. Fyodor Dostoevsky, *The Brothers Karamazov* (New York: Penguin, 1982), 124.

9. C. S. Lewis, *Prince Caspian* (New York: HarperTorch, 1979), 146.

10. Ibid., 148.

CHAPTER 4: FROM BEAUTY TO WONDER

1. Abraham Joshua Heschel, *I Asked for Wonder: A Spiritual Anthology*, ed. Samuel H. Dresner (New York: Crossroad Publishing, 1983), vii.

2. Ibid., 3.

3. J. H. N. Sullivan, cited in Richard Harries, *Art and the Beauty of God: A Christian Understanding* (New York: Mowbray, 1993), 92.

4. Robert C. Fuller, *Wonder: From Emotion to Spirituality* (Chapel Hill, NC: University of North Carolina Press, 2006), 15.

5. Roger Friedman, "Heath's Bad Habits Worse than Thought," Fox News, May 18, 2015, https://www.foxnews.com/story/heaths-bad-habits-worse-than-thought.

6. Blaise Pascal, *Pensées: The Provincial Letters* (New York: Random House, 1941), 134–35.

7. Augustine, *The Confessions of St. Augustine*, trans. John K. Ryan (New York: Image Books, 1960), 1.

CHAPTER 5: FROM WONDER TO WORSHIP

1. This story is quoted in Phillip Ryken, *Ecclesiastes: Why Everything Matters*, Preaching the Word (Wheaton, IL: Crossway, 2010), 54–55.
2. "1392. Doxazó," Strong's Concordance, Bible Hub, accessed May 24, 2022, https://biblehub.com/greek/1392.htm.

CHAPTER 6: ENJOYING GOD IN WHAT HE MAKES

1. Maltbie Babcock, "My Father's World," in *Thoughts for Every-Day Living* (New York: Charles Scribner's Sons, 1901).
2. George Marsden, *Jonathan Edwards: A Life* (New Haven, CT: Yale University Press, 2003), 44.
3. Mike Mason, *Champagne for the Soul: Rediscovering God's Gift of Joy* (Colorado Springs: Waterbrook Press, 2003), 26.
4. Nicodemus of the Holy Mountain, cited in Ann Voskamp, *One Thousand Gifts: A Dare to Live Fully Right Where You Are* (Grand Rapids: Zondervan, 2011), 102.
5. "Finite realities, such as . . . a tree, or a mountain, can be taken as points of departure for the ascent insofar as each of them, in its own way, mirrors God as the creator—and therefore also, in some sense, shows God to be the 'formal cause' . . . of all things. In concentrating on the tree [for example], . . . we can discover certain traits in it that suggest an essential reference to its first cause, and thus, by way of conclusion, direct the mind to God. Having found God . . . the mind can then enjoy its discovery by realizing that the reference of finite realties to God entails a certain presence of God *in* those realities, not only behind them or deep down . . . but also *in* and *as* their ultimate and primordial truth and 'essence.' God's infinite being then becomes visible, audible, touchable, as displayed . . . in the mirror of finite entities." Adriaan Peperzak, "Platonian Motifs in Bonadventure's *Itinerary of the Mind to God*," in *Christian Spirituality and the Culture of Modernity: The Thought of Louis Dupré*, ed. Peter J. Casarella and George P. Schner (Grand Rapids: Eerdmans, 1998), 57; quoted in James Fodor, "The Beauty of the Word Re-membered: Scripture Reading

as a Cognitive/Aesthetic Practice," in *The Beauty of God*, ed. Daniel J. Treier, Mark Husbands, and Roger Lundin (Downers Grove, IL: InterVarsity, 2007), 174–75.

6. John Piper, *When I Don't Desire God: How to Fight for Joy* (Wheaton, IL: Crossway, 2004), 184–85.

7. Cited in John Piper, *The Pleasures of God: Meditations on God's Delight in Being God* (Colorado Springs: Multnomah, 2000), 95–96.

8. Thomas Dubay, *The Evidential Power of Beauty: Science and Theology Meet* (San Francisco: Ignatius Press, 1999), 77.

9. Clifford Pond, *The Beauty of Jesus* (London: Evangelical Press, 1994), 42.

10. C. S. Lewis, *God in the Dock: Essays on Theology and Ethics*, ed. Walter Hooper (Grand Rapids: Eerdmans, 1970), 280.

11. "How Great Thou Art," Swedish poem written by Carl Boberg in 1885, translated by Stuart K. Hine in 1949.

CHAPTER 7: ENJOYING GOD IN WHAT WE MAKE

1. Michael Card explains, "Remember that only God can imagine and make something out of nothing. In this sense, he is the only One who deserves the title of Creator. We are merely creative." Michael Card, *Scribbling in the Sand: Christ and Creativity* (Downers Grove, IL: InterVarsity, 2004), 122.

2. Pablo Picasso, quoted in Robert Cumming, *Art Explained: The World's Greatest Paintings Explored and Explained* (New York: DK Publishing, 2007), 98.

3. John Calvin adds, "Whenever we come upon these matters in [non-Christian authors], let that admirable light of truth shining in them teach us that the mind of man, though fallen and perverted from its wholeness, is nevertheless clothed and ornamented with God's excellent gifts. If we regard the Spirit of God as the sole fountain of truth, we shall neither reject the truth itself, nor despise it wherever it shall appear.... We cannot read the writings of the ancients on these subjects without great admiration. We marvel at them because we are compelled to recognize how preeminent they are. But shall we count anything praiseworthy or noble without recognizing at the same time that it comes from God?" *Institutes of the Christian Religion*, trans. John Allen (Philadelphia: Presbyterian Board of Publication, 1843), 2.2.15.

4. C. S. Lewis, *Christian Reflections*, ed. Walter Hooper (Grand Rapids: Eerdmans, 1967), 10.

CONCLUSION

1. C. S. Lewis, *The Last Battle* (New York: HarperTrophy, 1984), 212. Here is the rest of the quote in which Lewis comments on the feelings of the Narnians as they discover the new Narnia and realize the old Narnia was merely a shadow of it: "It is as hard to explain how this sunlit land was different from the old Narnia as it would be to tell you how the fruits of that country taste. . . . [The new Narnia is] deeper, more wonderful, more like places in a story: in a story you have never heard but very much want to know. . . . The new one was a deeper country: every rock and flower and blade of grass looked as if it meant more. I can't describe it any better than that: if you ever get there you will know what I mean. It was the Unicorn who summed up what everyone was feeling. . . . 'I have come home at last! This is my real country! I belong here. This is the land I have been looking for all my life, though I never knew it till now. The reason why we loved the old Narnia is that it sometimes looked a little like this one.'"

2. J. I. Packer, *Concise Theology* (Wheaton, IL: Tyndale, 1993), 267.

FOR MORE TEACHING RESOURCES FROM PASTOR STEVE DEWITT

THE JOURNEY

The Journey is Pastor Steve's radio, podcast, and online resource. For more information, go to **thejourney.fm**. You can also find *The Journey with Steve DeWitt* on most popular podcast stations.

Steve has served in northwest Indiana as Bethel Church's senior pastor since 1997. The church website houses years of messages and resources. You can access these at **bethelweb.org**.